PRAISE FOR <u>WHERE TO?</u>

"Funny, touching, observant, philosophical, sad, world-weary, artful and wonderful are the stories that pepper this book. There has never been a cab driver like Dmitry Samarov and, since he's given up for keeps late-night for-hire driving, there never will be." —Rick Kogan, hall-of-fame reporter for the *Chicago Tribune*

"With his gorgeous pen and ink drawings and funny, tragic, and all too true stories, Samarov's chronicle of his adventures as a Chicago taxi driver is by far the best ride you'll ever take in a cab."
—Wendy MacNaughton, author and illustrator of *Meanwhile in San Francisco*

PRAISE FOR <u>HACK</u>

"Samarov captures the most shocking and, sometimes, quietly poignant tales. . . . When chatty barflies, clandestine drug buyers, inebriated sports fans, and prostitutes mentally preparing for johns pour out to their cab driver on a nightly basis, the truth is stranger than fiction." —*TimeOut Chicago*

"[Samarov's] book, organized by the days of the week, is thin and enveloping, full of the kind of insights only a veteran cab driver would have . . . The book is also so attuned to the nuances of cab life, a thought repeatedly springs to mind as you read it: Your cab driver is aware of you. More than you realize." —*Chicago Tribune*

"Samarov drives late afternoon and into the night, the best time to cull material to create his vibrant, detailed stories that would make Nelson Algren proud. He has that very Chicago knack for succinctly capturing the city's neighborhoods and the characters that inhabit them." —*Chicago Sun-Times*

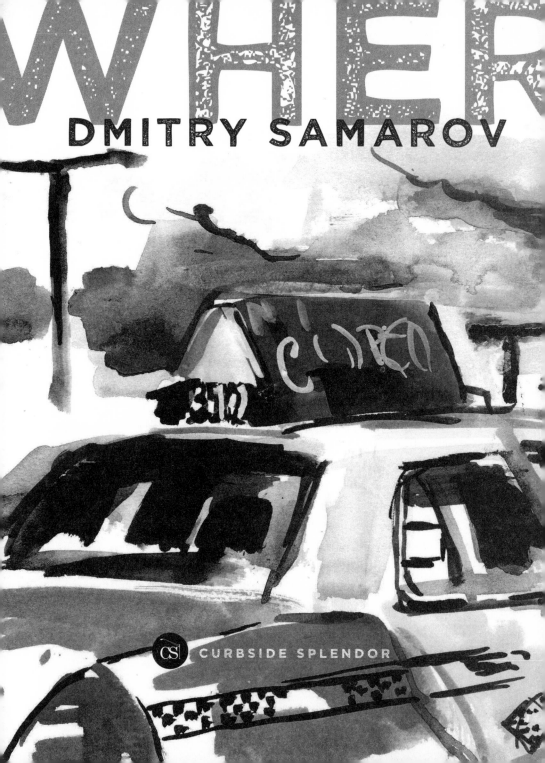

CURBSIDE SPLENDOR PUBLISHING

Published by Curbside Splendor Publishing, Inc., Chicago, Illinois in 2014.

First Edition
Copyright © 2014 by Dmitry Samarov
Library of Congress Control Number: 2014945091

ISBN 978-1-940430-22-5
Edited by Naomi Huffman
Cover and interior art by Dmitry Samarov
Designed by Alban Fischer

Manufactured in the United States of America.

CS

www.curbsidesplendor.com

CONTENTS

About All This Art / 7

1. First Ride / 11
2. Rules & Regulations / 23
3. Out-of-Towners / 45
4. Holidays / 55
5. Suspension / 69
6. Good Ones / 79
7. Bad Ones / 99
8. Romance / 115
9. End of the Night / 131
10. Regulars / 145
11. Last Ride / 157

Some Notes / 175
Afterword / 185
Acknowledgments / 187

My first book, *Hack: Stories from a Chicago Cab*, took a look at a driver's typical work week. This one, which begins with my first fare as a 23-year-old cab driver in Boston and ends with my last fare as a 41-year-old cab driver in Chicago, is more of a summing up of all my time behind the wheel. Between the first and last rides, the episodes are arranged thematically rather than chronologically in an attempt to give a sense of the breadth of experiences in my twelve years on the job. There are still many small moments—watching and listening to people is at the root of everything I do—but unlike the first book there's a beginning and an end and thus an opportunity to look back.

I never intended to write a thing.

When I decided to write about driving a cab, I needed a way in. That way in was through drawing. I don't ever remember not drawing—it's how I talk to the world—so, although it's probably not how most people would ease their way into writing a book, I didn't know of any other way.

The pictures I've included are culled from posts from the last two years of my blog, *Chicago Hack*, as well as the *Hack* zine from 2000, and sketches I did in the cab over the years while waiting at airports and cabstands. Drawing and painting are still my surest way into writing. While I'm finishing a picture, the phrases I'll use crystallize in my mind. And as I'm writing, I'll look back at the artwork to remind myself of the scene I'm trying to render in words.

The artwork in these pages runs the gamut from on-site, observed sketches to atmospheric, remembered city scapes to flat-out caricatures. Almost every piece of writing I've ever done has started with a drawn or painted image of some kind. The kind of picture it is depends on what I'm trying to write. Sometimes it complements the text, other times it serves as a counterpoint, but in every instance one can't exist without the other.

Because of the prohibitive costs of color printing, I restricted the illustrations for these cab stories to black-and-white. Some were done with ballpoint pen or charcoal, but most of the art in this book was done with Sumi ink. At this point, I've been working with it for about 17 years. It has the richest tonal range of any ink I've tried.

The painting on the cover of this book is *O'Hare Taxi Staging Area #1*. It's the first of a series of gouache paintings I did at Chicago's airports while waiting to be dispatched to the terminals to pick up fares. The challenge was to finish the painting before my subject matter left. The taxi staging area is a big parking lot where cabs line up in rows. Once the starter radios for cabs, the rows move out. At the outside, I had about three or four hours to get down in brushstrokes as much of what I saw as I could. Out of the 40 or so of these that I attempted, about ten or fifteen came out okay.

O'Hare #23 (pg. 7) is one of the dozens of ballpoint pen sketches I did over the years at the airport. These sketches were never meant to be preparatory studies for more finished work. They were always an end in themselves. I've chosen to use several of them throughout this book to give a sense of what cab drivers spend much of their day looking at: other cabs.

Dispatch Squawk (pg. 11) was one of my first attempts to illustrate what it was like to be a cab driver. It was painted for Hack #1 in 2000. The words and numbers shooting out of the two-way radio were meant to convey the nonstop cacophony throughout the long shifts.

Empty Lot (pg. 19) was one of the first times I used Google Streetview as a visual reference for an illustration. I needed to see one of the places I was trying to write about that was no longer there and sure enough, Google had a recent record of it. This particular lot was on California Avenue, just past the Kennedy Expressway, the former home of the worst cab garage from which I had the misfortune of renting a vehicle.

Cabbies #3 (pg. 32) was done while sitting through one of the interminable refresher courses the city requires drivers to take. I've done sketches of classmates and teachers ever since elementary school. For most people, sitting in a classroom means taking notes, listening, or sleeping; for me it has always been time for drawing.

Sometimes I needed a picture that wasn't that specific, but more of a general notion of what I was trying to write about. *Business* (pg. 45) depicts a series of office types with roller suitcases. It's the sort of sight that's ubiquitous in any city, but by taking the time to paint I was able to focus on the words I needed to say what I needed to say.

Blizzard (pg. 61) gave me a way to communicate the feeling of being enveloped in snow in a way that words could not. When writing works it's able to put you in a particular place, but oftentimes, a few accurate ink marks will do it even better.

When two 20-year-olds spend a whole ride talking about *Charles Bronson* (pg. 85), it made what I was going to paint a no-brainer.

Many of the portraits of passengers—like *Braggart* (pg. 106)—were done from memory and, often, not exactly meant to flatter. But others—like *Tony Fitzpatrick* (pg. 152)—were done from life and were meant to depict people the best I could. It all depended on the tenor of the ride and what I was trying to tell about the person. Some were character assassinations while others were faithful, straightforward depictions. I met all kinds and tried to render as full a spectrum as I could.

My first impulse has always been and will always be to reach for the brush before the pen. The words in this book would never have been written if I didn't draw or paint them first. I take the world in through my eyes best and there would never be any words without these pictures.

BOSTON

've met very few cab drivers who set out to be cab drivers. In 1993, I was an art-school graduate in Boston looking for a job. I wasn't interested in art-related employment but hoped to try something other than a restaurant or retail gig. I'd learned to drive only a year before but that new skill allowed me to widen the scope a bit. My search led to a seedy office inside a garage on Saint Botolph Street, the headquarters of Checker Taxi Company of Boston. A shifty-eyed old man explained that I'd need to take classes at Jamaica Plain High School, pass a multiple-choice exam, get a Hackney Carriage license from the Boston Police, then come back to see him with $200 in hand for a deposit.

The guys in that high school classroom came from all over the world. Most were recent immigrants trying to get a foothold in their new country. All of them seemed much older than me; doctors, lawyers, and teachers in the old country, forced back down to the bottom rung of the societal ladder in the new. All we had in common was being from elsewhere and wanting this strange job to get us where we wanted to be. I became a cab driver a couple weeks later.

My first fare was a businessman in Copley Square who wanted to go to Logan Airport. I had no idea how to get there. He had to give me directions and was none too happy about it. I don't remember if he left any tip aside from the advice to figure out what the hell I was doing. A couple months later I let a prostitute sit up front because she claimed she was cold. She found my wallet under the armrest with a whole night's earnings, some $200, and disappeared without even paying the fare on the meter. These and other lessons were tough, but I eventually got the hang of it. I liked discovering the city, seeing all of it in ways I never could have as a kid growing up in the Boston area. I'd held jobs at the Coolidge Corner Theatre, Edibles restaurant, and Kupel's Bagels, all within a mile-long stretch of Harvard Street in Brookline—not exactly a representative sample, and much less a microcosm, of the world I saw from behind the wheel of a taxi.

I met other drivers. A smooth-talker named Kenny, who always had some new get-rich scheme going, like the one I remember about a book teaching women how to get men to love them; an older Welshman named John, for whom driving a cab was but the most recent in a lifetime of odd and varied modes of employment; a middle-aged family man named Gene, who worked days as a fireman and would often have me drop him at the firehouse to sleep after a shift behind the wheel. There was the amped-up New Yorker who'd horrify his fares by happily saying, "We'll go through the windshield together, baby," when they voiced their misgivings about his driving. He'd also refer to black people, obscurely, as "The Demographic." There was a female driver who most of the guys wouldn't dare cross. She was one of the old-timers, the remaining few still working for the company on commission. This meant she split her earnings 40%-60% with Checker and received benefits; the rest of us had to pay our daily or weekly leases at the end of the shift, whether we'd made a dime or not.

The whole thing felt like an adventure to a guy in his twenties. I even developed a sort of persona, wearing a black Stetson and a leather jacket. Customers would try to guess where I was from, coming up with anything from Texas to the Midwest, none coming up with Moscow, USSR. I drew self-portraits in the rearview mirror while waiting at cab stands, none recognizably the same person. I'd usually work on my paintings—mostly views out the window or inside my small studio apartment on Commonwealth Avenue in Brighton—before picking up the cab at the garage for the 4:00 p.m. – 4:00 a.m. shift I drove six or seven days a week through most of my Boston cab career.

The job had its perks. I liked being able to take breaks whenever I wanted to go see bands at the Middle East or movies at the Coolidge. I liked not having to answer to anyone and trying to make my own luck to earn a living. But in the end Boston got me down. I'd never cared for the place growing up—my family emigrated from the Soviet Union in 1978 and I stayed through high school graduation in 1989.

I wasn't making many friends and I was drinking too much, so I moved back to Chicago—where I had gone to college—in 1997.

TAXI DRIVER

When I began driving a cab in fall of 1993, *Taxi Driver* provided my first frame of reference. As I drove through steam coming up from manhole covers, the image of Travis Bickle's hulking Marathon doing the same in the movie's first shot would start in my head, Bernard Herrmann's score surging as if out of nowhere to follow my taxi down the nighttime streets. When smartass college kids asked if my job was like the show *Taxi*, my comeback was always, "No, it's more like the movie *Taxi Driver*." They'd either laugh nervously or get really quiet after that. But it wasn't Bickle's need to cleanse the world through biblical bloodletting that attracted me; it was that tank of a car rolling through the city. A cab driver sees the ugly, the beautiful, and the just plain inexplicable as few others can. Being a passing presence in dozens of lives a day leaves its mark. I took Bickle's "I go anywhere, anytime," as a modus operandi.

When I say I'm inspired by the film, people often get a worried look. Read literally, of course, what Bickle does is insane, but no one should take it as a call to action (unless your plan is to kill Ronald Reagan to prove your love for Jodie Foster, of course). After seeing the movie again recently with a bunch of friends, a spirited debate continued all the way to the bar. The question: Is Bickle just crazy? One of the guys in particular insisted that no sane person would ever take a girl to a porn theater on a first date and think it was okay. He couldn't accept much of the plot as believable in any way. My take has always been that the character isn't just some guy and the story's not a slice of life. This is a man who talks about a rain coming and washing the streets clean of scum, of his life just needing a sense of a place to go. He's trying to save us all. Given that director Martin Scorsese trained for the priesthood and screenwriter Paul Schrader was brought up in a Calvinist household, it's no surprise that they'd make a movie about a fallen angel or holy fool. He sees the world as ugly and wants to make it beautiful. He never seems to get anyone's jokes, he doesn't connect with anyone else. "I'm God's lonely man," he says. Betsy's the Madonna figure and Iris is the whore; these and other characters are archetypes rather than real people. I never identified with Bickle, apart from sometimes sharing his loneliness.

A man alone, hurtling through nighttime streets in a taxi, all kinds of humanity passing past the windshield: now *that* I'm familiar with. There's a scene where a passenger (played by Scorsese) describes in detail how he's going to murder his philandering wife. I had a drunk tell me once that he had no money for the fare and that he was going to go into the house and kill his wife. He wanted to know what was I gonna do about it? I told him to do what he wanted but to get out of my cab, he'd wasted enough of my time. There's often no proper way to react when a stranger unburdens himself in this way. *Taxi Driver* gets the odd, fragmentary relationship between driver and passenger just right.

I got to know Boston and then Chicago the way Bickle got to know New York. I've never felt the need to save a soul, much less all our souls, but I wouldn't have gotten behind the wheel without his example. The job puts you at a remove from others and only certain types of people appreciate that sort of isolation. It always fit me to a T. At the end of the film, after the massacre and after he's hailed as a hero, Bickle's back in the cab, outside a hotel, waiting for a fare. Whatever happens to a cab driver, sooner or later it's always back to that wait, sitting and hoping for that fare that will take him away.

CHICAGO

I stopped at the Marathon gas station at Belmont and Western for a coffee and to use the facilities. The coffee was free for cab drivers after midnight. The car wash was as well. Out front, a mustachioed hack puffed out his gut and quoted the Bible to illustrate his travails behind the wheel to the clerk, who made a show of paying attention while smoking his break cigarette. I drove away without absorbing much of his wisdom except to note how much the place had changed.

Ten years earlier, when I tended bar at the Blue Light just up the street, a couple of the regulars worked for American United Taxi. Their offices and dispatching center were housed in the triangular building that came to a sharp point at the southeast corner of Belmont and Clybourn. There had even been a diner on the ground floor called The Point at one time. Eric was a grossly overweight dispatcher who'd play video poker at the bar for hours, drinking nothing but Diet Cokes. Timmy was a driver who'd pop in several times a night during most of my shifts. He'd slam a short Old Style and go back to his cab, which he'd parked haphazardly under the viaduct. On many of his visits, he'd try to mooch free ones from me or one of the barflies. His face was often scraped up or speckled with dried scabs and scratches, as if, to spare his taxi's tires, he had taken some of the brunt of the road's asphalt.

Bartending didn't suit me because I couldn't pretend to care or keep up the banter for eight hours a night, so in 2003 I went back to driving a cab. I put down a $200 deposit with American United, choosing it because I knew where they were headquartered. The cabs were dispatched from the back of the Marathon station. I signed on for the day shift, 6:00 a.m. to 6:00 p.m., so I could spend time with my then-wife in the evenings. Most of the drivers seemed to be grizzled, old, and white. They were still operating with two-way radios and each dispatcher had his own particular way that he demanded the calls to be read back to him. I didn't stick around long enough to master their system. The night man regularly returned our shared cab hours late and was rarely penalized, and the company wouldn't compensate me for the time lost.

The time they pulled me off the street in the middle of rush hour for an hour-and-a-half oil change was the last straw. I took back my deposit and went to Chicago Carriage, then to Checker.

Working for those other companies, I found out that there was plenty of business on the South and West Sides of Chicago. These were areas that American United shunned for the most part. Many of the American United drivers I'd encounter around town were of the disgruntled, dispossessed variety. A bit like Jim Ignatowski—the character Christopher Lloyd played on *Taxi*. Some of them looked like they lived in their taxis, others would tell odd, fantastic tales without much prompting. They were relics and I was glad not to be aligned with them.

In 2011, Yellow Cab bought American United, as it had bought out Checker a few years before. They remodeled the Marathon station, advertising free car washes and coffee for cab drivers, signaling a new era. There'll likely always be crabby old white guys driving taxis. They won't have a home at American United anymore though; it's just a brand name, the way Taco Bell is a subsidiary of PepsiCo. No cabs are dispatched from there; I hear they're all owner-operators now. I won't miss the way the place used to be. I like the way it is now: I pick up my free joe, take a leak, and leave. That old American United is best left in the past.

EMPTY LOT

Now that I don't drive anymore, thinking about all things concerned with cab life becomes a matter of recollection, especially in terms of places that are long gone.

Coming up the State Street ramp off the Stevenson, a field of haphazard grass and weeds comes into view. I do a double take because

thing doesn't seem right, then remember that the Harold Ickes Homes were demolished the year before. All that's left is an empty field. When landmarks suddenly vanish, it throws one off.

A few months after I started driving a cab in Chicago, I began commuting to Chicago Carriage Cab at 26th and Wabash to pick up my vehicle. This entailed taking the #49 Western bus, transferring to the #21 Cermak, then walking south, past the Ickes Homes, to 26th Street. It was an ugly, deteriorating project and the men who hung around the entrances of its buildings didn't exactly make passersby feel welcome. I don't scare easily, but the five minutes that it took me to cover those few blocks every morning were never my favorite. The last of these buildings are gone—likely to be replaced by more upscale housing—and knowledge of lives lived there will fade away. My connection to Ickes is tenuous, yet when I drive through the area and don't see those buildings, it gives me pause. What happened to the people who occupied the houses for all the years that they stood?

* * * *

In 2004, I briefly leased taxis from a garage on the 2900 block of North California Avenue, just past the Kennedy Expressway. Among the episodes that contributed to my abbreviated stay there was the time the owner accused me of stealing a water pump from one of his beaters. Said water pump had fallen off somewhere on the Eisenhower while I was attempting to ferry a businessman to the western suburbs. I was able to deliver him to his destination somehow, then waited for hours for the company tow truck to come rescue me. Back at the garage, my account of these events did not satisfy the boss; he decided instead that sabotage had to be the explanation. Another time, after three passengers in a row complained of smelling gas in the back seat, I had to take the car back to the garage before it blew up or poisoned its occupants. I don't remember many cabs from that garage that actually made it through an entire shift without something going at least a little wrong.

The place was leveled several years ago. Beyond a chain-link gate weeds have begun to break through the concrete where the garage once stood. The Citgo station just south of the lot is gone too; without the 24/7 parade of taxis to keep its pumps flowing, it probably wasn't a viable business.

* * * *

At the corner of Paulina and Warren Boulevard, there used to be a brick building that was originally owned by Red Cap Valet. It housed Checker Taxi for a couple years, until that company was absorbed by Yellow Cab. The building is no longer there, the space it occupied now just more satellite parking for the United Center, which sits a couple blocks southwest of it. I spent significant time going in and out of that place. Paying my leases, slipping the keys of my cab through the mail slot after hours, pacing back and forth by its locked door while waiting for the morning cashier—who had overslept—to arrive so that I could start my workday.

These and so many other such structures in this city are no more. They aren't significant or unique architecturally—nor in any other way for that matter—but their absence makes reconstructing memories that much more precarious and unreliable. The parts they played and the impact they had is debatable, but without them, there's that much more empty urban space full of questions.

ab drivers suffer many mundane indignities but few can match the obstacle course the city creates in order for us just to earn our daily wage. Phantom tickets, regulations on top of regulations, mandatory yet wholly worthless classes, you name it and they do it to us. New technologies are introduced to "make things easier." Taxi TV, new models of cars, and endless alterations to the credit card systems benefit and hinder the driver in almost equal measure. Add a newly-elected mayor trying to make his mark and what you've got is a work environment no sane citizen would envy.

AN OPEN LETTER TO
MAYOR RAHM EMANUEL

TO:

Office of the Mayor

121 N. LaSalle St.
Chicago City Hall 4th Floor
Chicago, IL 60602

I keep hearing about how you're planning to overhaul the city's taxi industry. Clearly there's plenty of room for improvement, but some of what you have in mind keeps me up at night.

You want to restrict the hours that a cabbie can drive per day, but that's one of the few freedoms we have: we choose when we work and when we don't. It's not a 9:00 to 5:00 job. Even if we wanted it to be, it doesn't pay well enough to justify those kinds of hours. It's a 24/7 business and it demands a workforce that can accommodate and bend with its ever-changing needs.

You want to better police reckless drivers as though all the tools to do so weren't already in place. Instead of adding more bureaucratic hoops for us to jump through, why not get the Secretary of State (that's what we in Chicago call the DMV) to join the 20th century (because the 21st would be a stretch). There's no reason that the Department of Consumer Services (which regulates cabs and cab drivers) shouldn't have access to driving records, for example. As it stands, every year when I renew my chauffeur's license I have to go back and pay twelve bucks for the cashier to push a button on her computer and print out my Motor Vehicle Record, then I have to carry it back to Consumer Affairs and present it to them. This is just one of a dozen superfluous steps in the yearly headache every Chicago taxi driver is subjected to for the privilege of continuing to earn his living. There's got to be some way to streamline the process a bit and let us get on with the task of getting by.

You want to know the kind of thing the police pull us over for over and over again? Let me share an anecdote: A few months ago I was stopped by an unmarked Crown Vic in Lincoln Park. The officer ticketed me because the little light over the license-display had gone out; two tickets—one of which I was to give to my cab company. He held on to my chauffeur's license, saying I'd get it back after I appeared in court.

At 400 West Superior a couple months later the court administrator kindly took pity and reduced my fine. When I asked for my chauffeur's license back he said they don't handle that, that I'd have to go to Consumer Services. So after an hour in court for a light bulb that went out I have to drive fifteen minutes and wait in another queue. This was all irritating and unnecessary but it didn't end there. Remember that second ticket—the one I had to give to my company? Well, guess what, I got to pay that as well! When a cab has equipment issues, the city gives one ticket to the driver and one to the company. According to my friend, the court administrator, it's to make sure they make the proper repairs but of course in practice the company just makes the drivers pay any and all fines. It's pay or go lease a vehicle from someone else. So I got to pay twice for a light bulb going out. About $200. Did that make the streets safer? Was my work environment improved? If you ask any veteran cabbie he'll have dozens of stories like this and much, much worse.

You want us to work less? Then raise the fare rates to at least keep up with the cost of living. As of this writing, cab rates have remained unchanged for six or seven years. I'm sure you know the statistics: Chicago has the lowest cab rates of any major city in America. I don't expect New York rates but we're killing ourselves for a pittance out there.

Some think the city should get out of regulating fare prices altogether. I don't. This is a unique business because we provide public transportation—an alternative to the CTA—yet are not city employees. In fact, we're no one's employees. All cab drivers these days are either owner-operators or independent contractors. Chicago's citizens deserve to have an idea what their ride will cost them. Leaving it up to the companies or individual cabbies would be utter chaos.

But that doesn't mean the city should micromanage our every move; we're not children. Ease up on the fees and nuisance traffic stops and give us a chance to get by.

Can you do that?

Sincerely,

Dmitry Samarov, cab driver
Chauffeur's License #84337

TRAFFIC STOP

One night I was taking a passenger home to Lakeview from Midway Airport and got pulled over for speeding. It was 9:00 p.m. or so and we were on Lake Shore Drive nearing North Avenue. There was a good amount of traffic. The cop lights came out of nowhere. Cab drivers develop a radar for cops the way dog owners develop a radar for dog shit but this one got the drop on me. Perhaps it was the pleasant conversation with the passenger that distracted me. He was as dumbfounded as I was at the officer's sudden interest.

The gray-haired officer marched up to my passenger-side window and asked, "Is there an emergency? Is your passenger going to the hospital?"

"No," I answered, trying to keep my voice as calm as I could.

"TURN THE METER OFF RIGHT NOW!" he bellowed, though I'd paused it the moment I saw those angry blue lights.

I had my driver's and chauffeur's licenses ready, as well as a bond card to hand over so as not to lose my license while the ticket was being processed. He took the licenses but sneered at the bond card.

"Don't bother. I'm pulling your chauffeur's license," he announced, and walked back to his cruiser.

The city has a special set of fines reserved for cab drivers. There's a room at the traffic courthouse at 400 West Superior just for us. This was where I'd be going in a month's time. In the interim every time I renewed my cab lease or had to show my chauffeur's license for any other reason I'd have to show the ticket instead. The shame of it was part of the punishment.

As we sat waiting the guy in the back told me he didn't understand what was going on.

"You didn't do anything wrong. In fact this is the calmest, safest cab ride I can remember. Don't the cops usually give you guys a break?"

I stifled a laugh and explained that cops hate cab drivers and that when ticket quotas need to be filled we're prime targets. We're out on the city's streets all the time. I was going with the flow of traffic. In fact another car had passed me right before the cop stopped me. He picked out the cab on purpose. The bright paint job and toplight must be hard to resist for the men in blue. I apologized to my passenger for holding him up. Before we were rudely interrupted he'd been telling me how tired he was from his trip and how much he was looking forward to getting home and having a beer. He just sighed and said he was sorry I was going through this.

When the cop came back his mood had lightened considerably. In fact, he was whistling a happy tune as he gave me the ticket and instructed me to turn the meter back on.

Later I went to 400 West Superior for my court date. The queue of sad sacks waiting to take their lumps was good and long by the time I arrived. The city has a lot of leeway with these cabbie infractions. Depending on the mood of the court administrator the charge can be dismissed or it can be upgraded to a suspension. The last time I was here—to pay twice for that light bulb that had burnt out—the administrator had recognized me from an article in the *Sun-Times* about my book. He asked that I not write about him and that the next time he'd give me a break. I brought a copy of my book in with me so he'd remember. He greeted me warmly and asked about how everything was going, saying that mine was a great story and that I should be on TV. He looked the book over, obviously impressed. I reminded him about his promise but he shook his head sadly as he looked at my ticket, saying there wasn't much he could do when it was for speeding on Lake Shore Drive, though he did knock the fine down from $250 to $125. I thanked him and went out to the courtroom to wait for the judge to make the deal official.

The judge read out my admission of guilt and handed me a document to present to the cashier, who relieved me of $165 ($40 added for "court costs") and sent me onto my next stop, the Department of Consumer Affairs, to retrieve my chauffeur's license. About an hour later I was at the Yellow Cab garage paying my weekly lease as if nothing out of the ordinary had occurred. The cashier took my IDs and cash without comment.

The police harassment and exorbitant fines are just the price of doing business. The city wants and needs revenue and we contribute.

After the extractions the city performed that morning, I looked forward to my dentist appointment later in the afternoon.

DRIVING LESSON

One of the requirements to renew a chauffeur's license—if one has incurred two or more moving violations during the prior twelve months—is a two-hour driving course. Harold Washington College is the exclusive local provider of these, at $125 per class. It was the prospect of this pleasure that found me at the corner of Lake and Wabash at 9:00 a.m. on a Tuesday.

An Indian fellow in his early thirties stands out front of the college, clutching the same registration papers as me, casting his eye westward down Lake Street. He's there for the same thing as I am, but is only at the very beginning of his cabbie career. The classes necessary to become a Chicago cab driver in the first place are also administered at this location. He bitches about the instructors, the fees, and the endless rules that have been drilled into his head, as we wait for our tardy instructors.

At 9:10, a compact car pulls up and a middle-aged man emerges slowly, opens the rear door and takes out a Driving School sign, then fastens it to the roof. I recognize him from the other time I'd had to pay this same penalty a few years back. He isn't exactly Mr. Personality, so it's a relief that he's come for the new guy, not me. After checking his student's paperwork, the teacher saunters across the street to Dunkin' Donuts. I stay there waiting for my prof to show up. A Toyota Prius appears a few minutes later and a scrawny, spiky-haired type gets out and repeats the older man's routine with the sign for the top of the car. He has me get behind the wheel and directs me to go up to Michigan Avenue and head south.

"Slow down," he commands as I push the needle past 20 MPH. When I point out that the vehicles behind us might like to get to their destinations before night falls, he says, "That's their problem," in an abrupt way. It takes herculean effort, but I manage to keep us under 25 MPH all the way to Roosevelt Road. We turn left, then wait at the stoplight to go south on Lake Shore Drive. I'm fool enough to attempt a right on red—which is fully permissible at this intersection—but the fact that I don't end up in the far-right lane after my turn brings a stern rebuke. Despite the fact that there's no one in the other lanes, he lectures me about proper lane usage. "You have developed bad habits," he chides. We crawl along the lakeshore well below the speed limit. Apparently satisfied, he opens a *Wall Street Journal*. We exit at Oakwood Boulevard and edge along in silence, apart from an occasional reprimand for actually hitting the brakes when trying to stop the vehicle. I know that engaging this pipsqueak would be a lost cause, so I bite my tongue. There are certain low-level jobs that attract controlling types. The piddling authority that they're given is wielded with a despot's restraint. To be a driving instructor can't have been his life's ambition, but my young master doesn't pass an opportunity to assert himself.

At around 10:00 a.m., we park at the turnaround behind La Rabida Children's Hospital for a break. The Indian guy and his instructor arrive a minute later. The teachers leave us alone, looking out at the lake. "He says I'm an aggressive driver," my new friend complains. I counsel him to just follow the directions, no matter how asinine. I say that I've forgotten more about driving than my teacher will ever know, which makes him laugh. He has many questions about the job. "How are you with the black?" he wants to know. When I say there have been no problems with the blacks, unbelieving, he adds, "Even at night?" I wish him well, as our instructors return from their own tête-à-tête, motioning for us to get back behind the wheel.

The glacial return trip back passes without much comment. He takes no notice of the long snake of vehicles behind us, looking up from his paper only to remark, "This economy is really messed up," to no one in particular. A few blocks from Lake and Wabash, he starts filling out an evaluation. My score is 93%. He hands it over, along with a certificate for completing the course. He reiterates my flaws as a driver then says to go up to the Professional Chauffeur Institute on the tenth floor to have all my paperwork signed. His next victim is already approaching the Prius as I thank him and cross the street.

There are many bureaucratic procedures involved in this business that all parties concerned know to be no more than revenue collection, yet we all play our parts because any attempt to question any of it will blow up in our faces. I appreciate the need to provide people employment. They give them documents to fill out and pass on to the next stop along the conveyor belt. Did spending $125 and two hours with this kid have anything to do with my aptitude for the job? Of course not, but without it, I'd no longer have the job.

CONTINUING EDUCATION

I arrive at Yellow Cab Headquarters at Cermak and Wabash at about 9:00 a.m. for the first of two city-mandated Driver's Safety classes.

Half the office staff seems to be outside for a smoke break. The teacher, Linda, who I remember from taking the class two years ago, is among them. This means that there's no hurry to get this thing going. Her strategy is to waste as much time as possible and end it as early as she can get away with.

The classroom is a windowless, stuffy chamber at the end of a hallway housing various departments. With all the doors open, a cacophony of conversations echoes up and down its length. Inside the room, there are four rows of tables with taxi meters and Gandalf terminals bolted at each seat. We sit facing a dry-erase board and a flat screen TV, filling out forms, while Linda sits at her desk in the back, coughing in the stale air. When she gets up to ask for our company IDs (to make sure we actually belong in this class) there's a guy who says he doesn't have his, claiming he's never been given one. Of course, seeing as one can't drive a Yellow without it, this isn't true and with a bit of encouragement he's persuaded to go out to his cab and retrieve it. Next, we're treated to a video about road rage. Although amusing for its unintentional industrial-film humor, I prefer the old ones that portray the consequences of reckless driving with blood and gore. In the discussion session that follows, a grizzled veteran in the front row opines that cabs should be equipped with sidewinder missiles to vaporize pedestrians. (Later, this same gentleman has to be roused from a slumber in his cab, as he's half an hour late getting back from our lunch break.) After we're all reassembled at around 12:00 p.m., we take a short quiz about traffic signs, hand over $2.45 to cover paper and printing costs, and are given our diplomas.

The following Tuesday I'm back in same room for the six-hour Continuing Education Class. This is a refresher course the city requires hacks to take every two years. Punctuality is just as optional as with the other class. We finally get going sometime around 1:30 p.m. The focus this time is more particular to cab driving. Linda asks drivers to share. The usual complaints about rude customers, merciless cops, and lousy business pour out of my classmates. This kills a good 45 minutes before movie-time. The video was made in 2002 and takes place in Florida. The gist of it is that courtesy's at the core of our profession. All well and good, but when I ask Linda why a more up-to-date film can't be shown, she explains that this one costs $300 a year to rent; to buy a new one would be even more. You'd think we were treated to a Hollywood spectacular rather than an amateurish industrial video.

After an hour meal break, Linda goes through a quick review of city regulations, geography, and a math problem in which we are asked to calculate mileage based on adding together city blocks and dividing by eight (there are eight blocks to a mile). She does it all with humor if little enthusiasm; before taking over all the driver classes at Yellow, she worked in the dispatch room taking calls, so perhaps dealing with us is easier than talking to the clientele. She explains that we have a two-part test to take and need 80% on both halves in order to pass. I'm first to finish and out of there an hour and a half early.

Thursday, my second Driver's Safety session is a copy of the previous week's with a couple exceptions: this time, an old geezer in the front row states that the reason he has to take this class is because he ran over a judge crossing the street downtown near the Daley Center (Miss Linda actually sits down to properly enjoy this story). Also, I'm handed someone else's certificate at the end of class and wind up having to pedal my Schwinn some five miles back to retrieve the correct one.

That's two mornings and one afternoon of my life wasted for no good reason (aside from the sketches I managed of my fellow cabbies).

There's gotta be a better way to make sure that cab drivers follow the rules.

SIDESWIPED

You never see it coming.

I'm in the turn lane on Michigan Avenue, waiting to go left onto westbound Chicago Avenue, when an SUV changes lanes and sideswipes my cab in the process. The SUV continues northbound through the intersection so I pull out after it, ignoring the light that had just turned red. A traffic aide—oblivious to what had just happened—bellows at me for ignoring the signal (no doubt a fly ticket to contest is in my future). But she can't be bothered to walk the twenty feet beyond Chicago Avenue, where I stop behind the offending Ford Explorer.

The driver of the Explorer is a young white woman who can't stop apologizing, "I'm SO sorry. I just moved here like, twenty minutes ago, and this happens." We exchange insurance information and I suggest that she follow me to the police station to file an accident report. She says she doesn't have the time, that she has to get back to her condo. "How far is Roosevelt?" she asks in parting.

"Two-and-a-half miles in the opposite direction," I tell her.

I go to the 18th District Station at the corner of Division and Larrabee, in the middle of where Cabrini Green used to be, by myself. The process of filling out an accident report is made exponentially easier when one has a sympathetic officer and there's no conflicting account offered by the other party; I have both these advantages. The desk officer sighs when I tell her that I'll likely lose a day of work over this at the very least. Any kind of damage to their vehicles is grounds for the cab company to send you home with no replacement car, nor compensation for time lost. This and other unpleasant possibilities crowd my mind as I drive south to my next stop.

I have to go to the Yellow Cab headquarters on Wabash, just south of Cermak, to file an insurance claim. The black lady who takes down my story has amazing hair. It's like a pile of glistening black-brown wood shavings piled artfully atop her head in an abstract sculptural arrangement. We spend more time talking about how her allergies are killing her today and how she just wants to get home to walk her pit bulls than about the mundane details of my fender-bender. She follows me outside to take pictures of the damage, bumming a Newport from the security guard on the way. "Oh, baby, that's nothin'. They can buff that out," she says, examining the streak that the Explorer left running from the right-rear quarter panel to the front passenger door of the cab.

I hope she's right. Any damage is an automatic $100 from a driver's deposit. No matter whose fault it is, they take it and don't reimburse until the insurance companies have had their say, months, sometimes years later. (I'm still waiting to be compensated for an accident that occurred in 2008.) My last stop is the cab garage, to hand over the accident report and find out how much more this will all cost me in money and time. I pull the cab inside and park it by the body shop. The manager insists on coming out and taking his own pictures. "I won't even charge you. They can buff that out," he offers generously. Watching the body guy squirt a viscous yellow fluid and work it into the side panel of the taxi with a spinning buffer, making the black skidding marks vanish, I thank the benevolent forces that spare me further misery on this day.

Two hours and a bit of running around. It could have been much worse. Lord knows it has been.

TALKING TOUCH-SCREEN

The call came at about 9:00 p.m. on a Monday night, just as I was walking out of the Music Box Theatre after seeing *Gun Crazy*. Lester, the night cashier, told me to show up at 3:00 a.m. to claim my car. No new cab leases are issued until that ungodly hour for reasons that have never been made entirely clear. I slept for an hour-and-a-half, setting the alarm for 2:00 a.m., then pedaled my bike through the sleeping streets to the garage. There were five or six drivers at the cashier's window and the bad news didn't take long to make it to the end of the line: they didn't have enough cabs for all of us. There had been several breakdowns overnight and those drivers were given replacement cars—the ones that were meant for us. When my turn came, all that was left was a handicap van. The cashier felt awful and promised she'd call as soon as a regular car came in. Her best guess was that it'd be around 7:00 a.m. or so. Going home to sleep would have virtually guaranteed that I'd miss the call and end up passed over for a legitimate vehicle for who-knows-how-long. There was nothing to do but to drive the van around and try to make a few bucks before dawn.

It took a long time to hook anyone in the early Tuesday hours. The one advantage of the van was that the middle row of seats was removed to make room for the wheelchair apparatus. This came in handy with the bicyclists I finally picked up. They were so high they could barely walk, let alone ride the rest of their way home. Both bikes fit, though getting both the guys to sit down proved a challenge; letting their limbs know what's required seemed to be a laborious task. After eventually settling in, they happily passed a cigarette back and forth and assured me that it was the greatest cab ride they'd ever had.

At 7:00 a.m., I traded in the van for a Crown Vic without even check-

ing it out and went home to get some sleep. I was back on the street by
1:00 p.m. As soon as the first passenger got in and I turned on the meter, an unwelcome jingle started up from the touch screen in the back of
the cab.

My first instinct was to go to TrueValue and get a hammer to silence
the squawking, but sadly, disabling the screen in this way would have ren-
dered the meter inoperable, seriously hindering my earning potential.

```
Want this squawking to cease?
Kindly press the RED OFF BUTTON
     (located at the bottom
         of the touchscreen)

Please do this for your own
sanity AND MINE...thanks
```

For two days, I told everyone who got in to press the red "OFF" button at the bottom of the touch screen to shut it up. Needless to say, it get
old fast. I was glad Yellow Cab had a new revenue stream, but listening
to Lionel Ritchie sing *Hello* a couple dozen times a day made me want
to drive into a wall, so the preventative measures I took were both necessary and inevitable. Until I could figure out what wire controlled the
sound on the damn thing to rip it out, I made a helpful card to communicate my humble request to the clientele. I was interested to see what
other drivers would do to combat this new threat to our sanity.

In the meantime, I was heading to Kinko's to have my sign laminated.

NO PARTITION

The taxi assigned to me has to go to city inspection. They promise to get it back to me on Monday. This means that I'll be driving a loaner until it comes back. The beater I get has too many problems to list; suffice it to say that I'm ready for a change come Monday, but by the afternoon there has been no phone call, so I drive to the garage to see what the problem is. At the cashier's window, I find out. Apparently "my" cab is actually someone else's and they took it back. No one bothered to tell me. Getting a straight answer out of anyone at the cab company is a rare feat and I don't accomplish it this day. They do have other cabs available, so it could be worse. After apologizing to the woman behind the glass for my profanity-ridden first reaction, I take the car key she offers and go outside to inspect my new ride.

Cab #1619 sits a few steps from the garage's entrance. It's a 2008 Mercury, unremarkable, except for one thing: it has no partition. I've driven cabs off and on since 1993 and have never had a vehicle without one. The bullet-proof partition is standard equipment, as much of a staple in a city taxi as a steering wheel, a meter, or lousy brakes. I'm truly thrown for a minute, sitting in the driver's seat and being able to reach and touch the back seat. I go back inside and tell the cashier I'll take it.

Partitions have been used in taxis since the late '60s. The thinking has always been that it deters potential muggers from attacking a cab driver. There are a couple problems with this idea: in order to actually hear where your passenger is going and to have a conversation with said passenger (if you're so inclined), the window must be open, thereby severely diminishing its bullet-stopping capacity. Also, if someone is bent on harming a cab driver, he can simply come at him from the driver's side window (and its flimsy glass). The partition reduces leg-room, which makes passengers more prone to being irritable. It reinforces the divide between "us and them" psychologically as well—but it's been there throughout my cab career.

I've never been physically attacked on the job. The hacks I've known that have been were all afraid. It's an animal thing to smell fear and a predator will always attack those that he can. I'm not naïve or reckless, but I've found that if you don't assume that a stranger wishes to harm you, they won't. Cab drivers are forced to make split-second value judgments every day. It's not that I always think the best of people (anyone who knows me will vouch to the contrary), only that if you treat a person straight, more often than not they'll treat you straight back. This is all to say that the fiberglass wall between me and the folks in the back has never made me feel protected, because I never felt I needed protection.

In the week that I drove Yellow #1619, I noticed a few things: I don't need to raise my voice the way I used to for passengers to hear what I'm saying. When paying up, they don't really know how much of my space to invade. Without the window, the space between us becomes nebulous; I often have to reach back to take the bills from their timid hands. I can also now see many more body parts when a couple is pawing at each other back there too. All in all, it was all right. The best part is that the touch screen (attached to the back of the passenger seat instead of being embedded in the partition) has no speaker. This means that I'm not subjected to that damn Walter E. Smithe Furniture commercial three dozen times a day and the sign I made, begging riders to turn the thing off, isn't necessary. It feels a bit more like I'm giving someone I know a ride, but only up to a point. I still have my back to them, I still don't know them and they still don't know me. There will always be a barrier whether there's a partition or not.

SCION

In the twelve years that I drove a cab, I had the dubious pleasure of dealing with a variety of vehicles. Cars with brakes that squealed so badly that by the end of a shift I felt like I had tinnitus. Cars with seats split so that I'd bring bits of padding with me (on the ass of my pants) every time I got out. Steering wheels so greasy from others' hands that mine would be blackened after a couple hours. Transmissions that would buck at every 10 MPH increase. None had fewer than 100,000 miles on the odometer until I got the Scion.

I had been renting cabs from the same garage for about five years. As in most places, those that cozy up to the management will get preferential treatment. In this case, it means primarily getting the newer cabs. They claim to have a seniority system, but their friends always get the cream of the crop and I've never been their friend. A couple weeks ago, I went out of town for vacation. Before leaving, I went into the office and asked Ken, the shop manager, whether there was any way he'd let me have the car I'd been driving back upon my return. He looked up my file on his computer and said, with surprise, "Well, you sure got enough time with us for that. But it looks like you take a lot of time off. I'm in the business of giving new cars to guys who won't drop 'em. Tell you what, poke your head in when you come back and we'll see what we can do." I thanked him without much hope for anything happening.

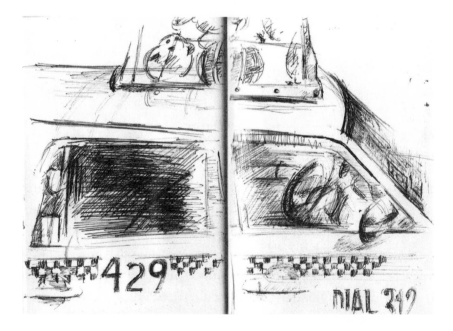

I came back to town and, after a day's wait, was assigned a cab. When asking whether there was any news, Ken answered curtly, "You're on my list." The car I got was far from the worst I'd had, but nothing to get excited about: a 2007 Crown Vic with 217,000 on the odometer and all the squeaks and aches you'd imagine of a machine of that vintage. I made it through four days before starting to daydream about the next chance to take time off, and then the phone rang. It was Ken, saying, "I got a brand new Scion. How soon can you be here?" I was at the garage in 20 minutes.

Transferring my receipts, street maps, Chauffeur's Guide, phone charger, pillow, and other gear into the Scion, it felt like moving into the corner office. This would mean paying a bit more in daily leases but saving at least $10 a day in gas; in a Crown Vic, I was lucky to get 10 miles to a gallon. I could also hook up my iPod into the stereo instead of using an FM adapter cable which made every tune hiss and crackle as if broadcast by a ham-radio operator. This cab even had that new car smell.

The weekend's passengers were impressed, many saying it was the nicest cab they'd ever been in. I had to tell them it was the nicest cab I'd ever been in as well. It had been my policy to allow smoking in the two years or so since I myself had quit, but I had to say no in this cab. Those that asked didn't put up much of a fight either. Perhaps because I've never owned many expensive things, it was odd for me to care about this new car's condition. This is probably how they get you: get something nice and going back to the broken-down crap you're used to is that much harder.

I'd stayed with this company all these years because they have more cabs than any other and I could take time off and reasonably expect there to be a cab for me when I returned. The Scion changed the game. Drivers and cashiers at the garage asked why I didn't have a regular car and my stock answer was that I liked to "date 'em, not marry 'em."

It was going to be difficult to give this one up. I was stuck, but at least I was stuck in comfort. If you saw Checker Cab #429 from March 2011 to June 2012, that was me.

Travelers and tourists are a different experience for a cabbie than the everyday local. They're often disoriented and on edge. Whether they're turned-around suburbanites or weary travelers, the task is to get them where they're going without scaring them or making them feel they got ripped off. It's not always so easy.

THE TOURISTS

I'm third in queue outside Navy Pier when two women approach tentatively. They want to take my cab, but I tell them it would be best to take the first one in line to avoid ruffling any feathers. They say they had a bad experience earlier and would wait for me, retreating to the doors of the headhouse. When my turn comes, they hurry back and get in. "Do you know of a chocolate factory nearby?" one asks. "We were on the boat tour and there was this wonderful smell and the tour guide said there was a chocolate factory nearby. We want to go there."

Their previous cabbie had asked them, "Do you want to meet God? He's at my house." This, understandably, made them wary of cab drivers in Chicago. They're relieved when I tempt them with nothing to match my colleague's offer. Pulling up to the Blommer factory at Kinzie and Des Plaines, one can only hope that they'll recall this sweet smell from our city, rather than the lunacy of some of our citizens.

THE RELUCTANT TRAVELER

An older black lady gets in at Midway Airport. She has to catch her breath before asking how much it will cost to a suburban bus depot some ten miles away. "I don't take cabs, but I just missed the shuttle and it's not called the Tri-State like I remember. They ought to tell you when they change the name like that. The lady told me it hadn't been called that in years. My son is picking me up there and going the rest of the way back to Hammond." When I tell her the estimate, she praises the Lord she'd won that $25 in scratch-off tickets: "He always looks out for me."

"You must be one of the lucky ones," I offer.

She's coming back from Atlanta where her daughter had moved. "They all gay in Atlanta. Don't know to say 'Yes, ma'am' or 'Yessir' half the time. They all wanna fake it, 'til they make it. My daughter got a short haircut and they told her, 'Better watch out, that's gonna attract them,' so she put in extensions. She told me it was bad, but I had to go see for myself...Just glad to be back in Chicago."

I tell her that I don't believe being gay is contagious, which makes her laugh but doesn't change her mind.

At the bus terminal, on the edge of a strip mall in Crestwood, I unload her matching floral print luggage and drive off, watching in the rearview as she looks around wearily, waiting for her son.

CORPORATE ITINERANTS

If you wait for a fare in the turnaround by Pioneer Court you watch for two things:

1.) Cop cars that will ticket for stopping at the curb (as this isn't a legal cabstand).
2.) Suits with rolling luggage in tow trudging across the plaza from 401 North Michigan Avenue.

It's worth risking the first to hopefully attain the second: a possible trip to the airport. Of course, more times than not, after you've loaded their suitcases into the trunk they'll announce that they're going to Clark and Lake. They choose the Blue Line train to O'Hare over a taxi in the early afternoon, likely thinking they'll get there faster and be able to fly standby on an earlier flight back. Many of them spend much of their lives in transit, switching from plane to train to car and then back, going into skyscrapers in one city or another, then gathering their things and moving onto the next city. I don't know what they're doing but I keep listening, watching, sometimes even talking to them, in the hope of getting some clue.

An older man settles into the back seat and says, "O'Hare," so we merge into northbound Michigan Avenue traffic. I hear him rustling around and making himself comfortable for the 45-minute ride. He's a talker. He starts with the weather, then moves on to describing his work. He travels the world marketing devices that measure pollutants in the air. He looks out at the Kennedy Expressway gridlock and estimates a number that doesn't sound good at all. He recalls measuring the mass of particles on a runway directly behind the engine of a jetliner: they were sequestered in a trailer with millions of dollars of high-tech equipment and weren't allowed outside because it was too dangerous—between the wind generated by the engine and the air quality.

"I did some back-of-the-envelope math and it looks like I've spent close to two full weeks just up in the air flying around this year. And I went down from Platinum to Gold this year. Guess I'm just used to traveling," he tells me, though it sounds more like he's just thinking out loud. At the Delta terminal he thanks me warmly and pays with a credit card, leaving $45 on a $40 fare. This isn't unusual: anything over ten percent from a suit feels like a victory.

At Midway an elegantly dressed gent asks to be taken to the Renaissance Hotel on Wacker. He spends much of the trip on the phone making appointments and barking out directives to a subordinate on the other end, all with a Southern lilt. By Soldier Field traffic halts due to an accident and he relates his annoyance at the delay into the cell. When he hangs up, just as we pass by a totaled sedan facing the pinched flow of inconvenienced motorists, he hears a snippet of the radio report about Occupy Wall Street and asks, "Y'all don't have any of that foolishness going on here, do you?"

"We do, in fact," I answer.

"It's crazy. We even had some of it in Nashville but it didn't amount to much." I make some sort of sound to acknowledge hearing his words. There's no way that we'll be discussing this subject. Not if we want to get to his hotel intact. A few minutes later we pull into the Renaissance's drive and he hands over a $50 and tells me to keep the change. The fare is only $30. Sometimes they'll shock the shit out of you, though maybe just keeping my mouth shut in this instance actually paid off.

A woman gets in at O'Hare's Terminal 2 and asks to go to Roscoe Village. Her first call is to a friend who had to have her cat put down. She tells her friend to come spend the night if she'd like and that she can be a cat for her instead, meowing to reinforce the point. "That'll get me a lot of dates, being into weird animal shit," she says, before hanging up. The next call is to a man and seems to straddle the personal and the professional. She goes to great lengths to set a time to meet him the next day, then starts talking about business matters, lapsing into corporate-speak. She wants him to show up at some meeting and pretend not to be her friend so as to avoid any appearance of impropriety. His marketing expertise would give her a leg up with the clients. There's something about trying to understand "verticals" and another thing about the "culture" of some office (though this sounds to me more like the bacterial kind of culture rather than the kind artists enrich people's lives with). I've had other business folk admit to loathing what their work does to the way they speak yet feeling powerless to just stop and talk like human beings to their colleagues. When we get to Belmont and Damen she thanks me—the only words she's aimed my way since leaving the airport—and leaves a 25% tip. Once more I'm surprised, as I've done nothing unusual to deserve her generosity.

I don't envy these corporate itinerants. I don't know whether what they do is of value to the world or not, but the glimpses of their everyday reality that I'm privy to don't make me want get out from behind the wheel. I keep picking them up in front of that hideous Marilyn statue (which stood in the middle of the plaza for what felt like years in 2012), or whatever eyesore replaces it, in Pioneer Court and from other office buildings around town, and keep hauling them onto their next appointment, wondering what it is that they're doing and why.

HOMELAND

Closing time at Damen and Division.

A young Hispanic guy with a buzz cut runs toward my cab from the Rainbo Club's sidewalk, where a half dozen exiled drinkers are pondering their next move. Most fares from the Rainbo at 2:00 a.m. end at the Continental, Estelle's, or an apartment nearby. After asking me to roll down the passenger-side window, the young man takes a deep breath and asks, "How much to take me to Aurora?"

I look in the *Chauffeur's Guide* to give him an estimate. This book—which contains listings of routes, fares, restaurants, hotels, and other useful info for cab drivers—is published and sold by a middle-aged, chain-smoking Middle-Eastern man whose name I've never caught. Many an afternoon he can be spotted with the latest *Guide* in hand, Marlboro hanging off his lip, going up and down the rows of cabs queued out at O'Hare or Midway. The book estimates the trip from downtown to Aurora at $110, so I tell the guy it'll be right around $100. He stands there thinking it over, then says, "All right, let's do this. You take credit, right?" I nod. He goes back to say goodbye to his friends then gets in the cab. We start south on Damen toward the Eisenhower. I explain that it's straight meter to the city limits and meter-and-a-half thereafter. He seems cool with that, asking again to make sure that I'll take plastic.

"I'm gonna tell you right now, I've got a gun. I work for Homeland Security. How often do cab drivers get robbed? Does that happen?" he asks.

"It happens," I answer, not knowing where he's going with this.

"Don't worry, man. I already told you I'm packin'. Hanging out with my cousin after work tonight and we stayed out drinkin' too long. I was really considering crashing at his pad but my wife had been texting all night. She wants me home. You know how it is. You married?"

"Divorced."

"So you know."

"If you love her there's no reason to start trouble. You're doing the right thing going home."

"Yeah, I love her. I've got a government vehicle but I usually take Metra in. I'm in no shape to be driving anywhere right now."

He falls silent somewhere past the Harlem exit on the Eisenhower. As with most suburbs, I know how to get to them but once out there I'm lost. The book says to take the Farnsworth Road exit so when I see it's a couple miles ahead, I glance back to rouse the kid, who's passed out, leaning forward with his forehead resting against the Taxi TV screen on the back of the seat. He looks around, disoriented, asking where we are and tells me after squinting about a few more seconds that we should've taken Route 59 a mile or so back. Seeing as he gave me no directions aside from "take me to Aurora" there's no way I could've known. Still, I ask how far off course we are and he says about five miles. I tell him I'll take ten bucks off his fare.

Off the highway now, we pass gas stations, fast-food restaurants, shopping malls and gated subdivisions with names like Stonemoor, Wood Edge, and multiple ones ending with -Haven, -Brook and -Shore. They all seem the same, unless it's the one you live in, I suppose. My passenger goes in and out of consciousness throughout this stretch so we end up making several more wrong turns before finally finding the subdivision he lives in. We settle on a total of $115 (which takes into account both my missing his exit and his failure to stay awake.) He hands over his card and just as I'm about to swipe it the system goes down. We're thirty-five miles outside the city so this isn't entirely unexpected. I wait a bit but there's nothing but "not receiving data" displaying on the terminal, so I take out a carbon slip from the glove compartment, lay it on top of the card, and rub my ballpoint pen over it to get an impression. It's faint and distorted, like music on a third-generation cassette, so I write out the numbers on the slip as well. I should really get a manual swiper but $35 seems a steep price to spend for a situation that only occurs when I'm out in the boonies, and rarely even then. He doesn't really know what's taking so long but is relieved when I hand him back his card. He shakes my hand and stumbles toward a darkened little house.

WRONG BALLPARK

It's 6:45 p.m. on a Monday as I arrive at Addison and Clark. Wrigley Field sits silent, free of the fans that glut these streets on a game night. Two girls in full-on White Sox regalia come running my way. I roll the passenger window down and one asks, "Are we close to Sox Park?"

"Nowhere near," I answer.

The game is starting in fifteen minutes and they're all the way across town. They ask if I can take them and I say, "Of course. It's what I'm here for." We make our way to Lake Shore Drive and turn south while they tell me how they ended up at the wrong ballpark.

"He dropped us off in front of Wrigley and that's when I started to think something was wrong. He was like, 'See? I get you here fast!' He didn't say sorry or nothing. We don't really know our way around the city too well."

He'd picked them up at Union Station and insisted on a flat rate of $20 when they asked to go to Sox Park. Not only had their cab driver overcharged them, but he'd taken them in the exact opposite direction.

"I think he went the wrong way down a few one way streets and he kept screaming at all the other cars while going 60 miles per hour. It was scary."

They'd come in from Naperville to meet some guys at the game. Instead they were now late and paying for a second (unnecessary) cab ride. I try to make them laugh about it. My opinion of their other driver is even worse than theirs. Guys like that make all of us look bad. I tell them to make sure and take down the cab number and call the city the next time they think something is off.

"Do they still charge full price if you show up to the game late? Our friends are already in their seats," one wants to know.

"Well, it's Monday, so it's half-price night already," I say.

"We know. That's why we came down."

I suggest they tell the guy in the box office their story and maybe throw in a few tears. What guy wouldn't want to help out two pretty girls? They laugh, saying they like that idea, telling me they know how to cause a scene.

We stop just past 35th Street on Wentworth so I can run their credit card. Their first driver refused to take it. I wonder whether the guy did anything right at all. They say this was their best cab ride ever. I thank them and suggest they call the city to let them know that as well. I watch them run to the park's gates. Not all cab drivers are crooks; some of us even know how to get to the right ballpark on the first try.

A concert, a holiday, or a snowstorm makes for a different kind of drive. Passengers are more grateful, more drunk, and more strange than on the average workday. People who don't come normally leave their houses come out on these days and it's the cab driver's job to get them back to their houses safe and sound and to get ourselves home in one piece as well.

In 1994, the Grateful Dead took over the Boston Garden for a week. Their fans set up a tent city for blocks around the stadium. I was driving a cab in Boston then and had the pleasure of carting these foul-smelling and entitled types around the town. For all the hippy-dippy peace-and-love espoused by the Dead's music, their acolytes tended to be passive-aggressive rich kids, likely slumming it before the old man kicked them in the ass and threatened to cut off the trust fund gravy train. A typical interaction would have one of them whining, "Hey, man, you're going the long way, man." Though it was his first time in the city. Jerry Garcia died the next year so I was spared further misery of this particular variety. In the case of the Dead, it's hard to say what was worse: their fans or their music. For other bands, the choice is far easier.

THE POGUES

In 2001, I went to the Vic Theater in Chicago to see Shane MacGowan of The Pogues play. MacGowan's is one of the most famed human garbage disposals of rock-n-roll, and on that night he didn't disappoint. Egged on by Irish-flag-waving fools, he threw up all over the stage (some poor roadie had to run out and mop up the mess) and unsuccessfully attempted to blunder through some of his own old songs. He was out of tune and completely out of sync with his backing band, who soldiered on the best they could anyway. I managed a sketch of MacGowan from the balcony at the Vic. It was one of the most pathetic and depressing things I'd ever seen, but the crowd ate it all up. I was a fan of The Pogues, but their best days were some 15 years in the past by then and seeing MacGowan debase himself on that night didn't help me to reminisce.

Ten years later, the reunited Pogues are in town to play the Congress Theater. The first people I drive to the show are two guys and a girl from Humboldt Park. They aren't wasted but they've definitely had a few. The thing about Pogues fans is that many seem hell-bent on outdoing their idols in inebriation and general debauchery. Most fall far short, but manage to be plenty ugly regardless. Aside from St. Patrick's Day, no other night will see more people in Irish-themed garb than the night of a Pogues show. Every Irish person I've ever met has had the highest contempt for what Americans have made of their holiday and the feeling of this night is very similar. Unfortunately for me, the rest of Chicago seems to have turned in early, so I have to return to the Congress again and again in order to make a living this night.

A girl steers her guy toward the taxi. He's in a kelly green newsboy cap and a T-shirt advertising the fact that he likes to drink. She gives an address in Lincoln Park and when we get to Fullerton and start going east, he perks up and asks if we're on Lake Shore Drive. She tears into him for making an ass of himself at the show: "That's why Kevin left, because you were being such a dick!" None of his responses are even remotely coherent. She pushes him out of the cab when we come to a stop, then apologizes several times before paying and stumbling away.

A tall bleached blonde flees the Congress next. She's from Ireland and loves The Pogues and all, but she's had enough. Ditching her friends, she asks to go through the Taco Bell drive-thru to put the night behind her. She spends the rest of the ride to Lakeview apologizing for her countrymen, as well as the honorary Irish of this evening. I have to roll all the windows down to free the cab of the Alpo stench of her meal while heading back west to the theater.

A weary woman waves me down on Milwaukee a block away from the epicenter of all the Irish insanity. There are cop cars all over the place because one of the revelers has apparently been struck by a car. As we drive north towards Albany Park, she tells me she waited 40 minutes for a cab. "I went out with my sister who goes out like once a year. She says she's gonna keep raging, I tell her I'm going home." She's in the music business, working with a band called Lucero, which is named after one of the saddest characters in movie history, a run down boxer in Fat City. "They're the saddest band in history," she says.

Returning one last time to the now-darkened and quiet Congress, I spot three people stumbling out of El Cid, a few doors down. It's the same three I started the night with. They're delighted at the coincidence. "You're the only white guy I know!" the girl states happily. She means the only white cab driver of course, but backtracks almost immediately, worrying that she's offended me. I tell her she's welcome to say whatever she likes, that it's between her and her god. The guys find this exchange to be the height of hilarity. The one sitting up front asks if I'm familiar with the work of George R.R. Martin. "*Game of Thrones*, right?" I say.

"Yeah. I told my fat pig of a sister to read it and she wouldn't do it. I highly recommend it," he answers. And with that they exit the taxi.

The shoppers have been out for the start of the seasonal feeding frenzy for many hours by the time I make it to Michigan Avenue. Traffic crawls as maddened hordes occupy all available space. Unfortunately it doesn't translate into many cab rides. Two hours in and there's hardly $20 to show for it. As evening nears, the streets empty, people perhaps still sleeping off the Thanksgiving meal from the day before. On certain slow nights a cab driver encounters characters that hide from the light the rest of the year. Black Friday is one of those.

I take the radio call on Washtenaw in Humboldt Park around 7:00 p.m. No sign of life for a few minutes, but then a kid with neck tattoos and a hoodie ambles up and motions that this friends would be right out. Two guys and two girls; the first guy sits up front with me. "Is this one of those freaky cabs?" a voice from the back calls out.

"Like *Cash Cab*?" I wonder.

"No, man, *Taxicab Confessions*, where they tell all the fucked-up shit they did, yo."

"Got something to share?" I ask.

This leads to a graphic discussion of all the positions that they'd do it in in the cab. I tell them it happens. The one in the front wonders if he could get his crotch up to the partition where his girl could have at it. They whoop it up when I tell them that there would be extra charges for that.

"By the way, yo, we're gonna kill you," he announces, dead-eyed, and tells his buddy in the back to hand him his knife. "Just playin'!" he cracks up. They get out at the Diversey Rock 'N Bowl.

The doorman at Rosa's Lounge, a blues club on the West Side, flashes his light to let me know he has a fare. A plump young blond comes out, followed by a guy in his 20s who's only still vertical because the wind has let up. She manages to finally lure him inside and we shove off for the Hotel Sax downtown. He mumbles to himself much of the way. The girl apologizes repeatedly, "It's my brother and he's really drunk."

"Really?" I ask.

When we arrive, she tries to get him to find his wallet without much luck. He gets out of the cab and comes up to the passenger-side window, attempting to form the few words that might help him puzzle out what's being required of him here. He keeps playing with his cell phone as if the right button will make this situation disappear. Finally, he stumbles to the ATM a few feet away to withdraw the fifteen bucks I've now asked six times for. The girl tries to explain that he's in the military and not to get mad, that she won't get out until I'm paid.

My pay is the least of the problems here, I tell her. "Your brother is an alcoholic and he's gonna come to a bad end."

"I know," she admits.

The next couple that gets in discovers a pair of black leather gloves in the back seat. I tell the girl that it's a Black Friday special where gloves are offered to all my passengers. She happily puts them on.

"Do people often leave things in cabs?" her guy asks.

With no apparent transition, the girl tells us, "Karl Malone was the first black man I ever saw. He came to a barbecue at my parents' house in Idaho."

I thank her for letting me know. When I pull into the drive of their Gold Coast high-rise, the guy tells me this has been the most enjoyable cab ride he can remember and tips accordingly.

A well-dressed woman hails me from the doorway of Tavern on Rush. In the cab, her husband rolls down his window and bellows at the top of his lungs to a fat guy in front of a white stretch limo, "MAN-

NY, YOU'RE THE PUERTO RICAN RON JEREMY!" To me and his wife, he says more quietly, "He really is," as we roll away from the Viagra Triangle.

Near their Lincoln Park home, the conversation takes an abrupt turn. The husband says, "Let me ask you, because me and my wife keep going back and forth on this: should we raise our kids in the city or just move to the suburbs?"

"Suburbs are a symbol that you've given up," I offer.

"Thank you! It's so nice to talk to a sane person," he beams.

"You don't know me that well, sir," I assure him.

The two girls get in at 4:30 a.m., just about the last fare of this long night. They're going from Wicker Park to 18th and Throop in Pilsen. One insists that I put on Lite-FM, which plays Christmas music 24/7 this time of year. To the soundtrack of "Silver Bells," the other girl announces, "All I want right now is a toilet bowl to puke in."

BLIZZARD

Every winter in Chicago the weather forecasters go overboard predicting epic snowfall and general end-of-the-world type storms. On February 1, 2011, for once, they weren't wrong. And I got to drive a cab through it.

I don't leave the house until about 3:00 p.m., and the snow has already begun falling. The trip northbound is a slog as office workers, released early, all try to get home at once. Starting the day's labors when everyone else is finishing isn't really that unusual. All the news hysteria about the coming storm isn't any deterrent either. I've loved the snow my whole life and the more the better, right?

It takes half an hour to take my first fare two miles north of where I'd picked her up. I try every side street detour I know to no avail. We get there eventually. An hour into the day, I've had to clear off the back window three times to make up for the nonfunctioning rear defrost (an all-too-common feature of our taxi fleet). Now that the radio is reporting on actual events as they happen, rather than predictions, I pay closer attention and stay off the highways. By about 6:00 p.m., the streets begin to empty of cars, their void filled with swirling, blowing white flakes. This allows my cab to fishtail freely, with far less chance of collision. A Mercury Grand Marquee is hardly the ideal vehicle for a blizzard; it's huge, low to the ground, and has rear-wheel drive. I can't see much more than 20 feet in front of me; the front window fogs up every time a new passenger gets in as well, and a cracked window and a wipe with a napkin can only do so much. The world cocoons me and fades to nothing at its edges.

This quiet is what I've always loved about the snow. It slows the city to a crawl and muffles its clanging. It reminds me of how small we are in relation to the world in which we live. While the actual steering of the vehicle is more of a challenge now, dealing with the clientele is virtually stress-free. People that are lucky enough to find a cab are absurdly grateful and overpay lavishly. I get many tips this night that are double or triple the meter fare. At about 8:00 p.m., one of these fortunate souls has me take him to an obscure and narrow side street named Race. Up until then I had not gotten stuck anywhere, but after dropping him off I try to continue west and start spinning my wheels 30 feet up the block. I reverse a bit and try to hit the one pristine-looking set of tracks ahead. It's soon clear the vehicle that made them did so awhile ago and they provide no traction. Some ten minutes of one-foot-forward-two-feet-back get me clear. It is now that it sinks in that this blizzard isn't like the other storms that have always seemed like such a breeze to me. I get stuck three or four more times before I start telling anyone that gets in that I don't do side streets.

The condensation problem gets to the point that I feel the need to actually do something about it. At the Yellow Cab garage, I explain my problem and the mechanic leans in, laughing, and turns a rigged knob hanging free just below the dashboard; the windshield is crystal clear in less than a minute. I had assumed that it was some vestige from before the cab company had customized this car and had no idea it actually served a purpose. This is one of those moments when I'm thrilled to look like a clueless idiot. I thank him and roll back into the snow globe outside.

At about 11:30 p.m., I'm worn out enough to think about calling it a night. My plan is to reward myself with a Kuma's burger but after sliding all over the Kennedy expressway for an exit or two, narrowly avoiding a few sliding 18-wheelers, I turn back and head homeward instead. Western Avenue is passable, though down to one meandering lane in each direction. The further south I go, the more darkened houses line my path. When I see the McDonald's M is unlit at the corner of Washington, I know there will be no power on at my house. Sure enough, it's a blackout for blocks around, but I never get to my front door because the drifts are so high that turning onto any side street to park is not wise. Leaving the cab on Western is an automatic tow, so the choice is to just drive all night or find other shelter. I call my girlfriend in Beverly to say I'm going to attempt to get to her house, and continue sliding south.

99th Street looks precarious, but I chance the left turn and slowly make it the mile or so east, mostly in what is normally the westbound lane. This street is part of the city's official snow route though (meaning I can't park here either), so one more turn is inevitable. It takes some 40 minutes for me to get the cab into something approximating a parking space. I look back at the path I'd cut through all that pristine white, then drag myself into the warm house.

I help shovel around the house the next day. Checking on the cab, it doesn't look too buried and the street it's on has been cleared so I take it easy until evening before digging it out to prepare to leave. At 8:00 p.m., I take a look inside and see the faint green glow of the Gandalf dispatch terminal. I'd left it on the night before and this means a certain dead battery. I call the dispatcher to send the tow truck; she tells me that she doesn't know how long it's going to take. There are hundreds of cars stranded on Lake Shore Drive, so a cab on the South Side needing a jump isn't the highest priority. The tow truck arrives around midnight, the driver looking like the walking dead; he says he hasn't slept in two days. The cab roars to life and I'm off.

It's remarkable to see all the major streets so clear. They're certainly narrowed by five-foot piles of cleared snow in many places, but 24 hours after one of the worst storms in Chicago's history, I can't help but be impressed. My first fare has been waiting for a cab for hours. She's going to a hospital in Marquette Park. She thanks me when I drop her at the ER and says, "I'll be calling you again."

FATHER'S DAY

A squat figure waves her cane my way at Milwaukee and Fullerton. She labors to climb into the cab, takes a deep breath, and asks to go to the 5700 block of North Clark. We drive east on Fullerton, then turn north on Ashland before she breaks the silence.

"How was your Father's Day?"

"You're looking at it. I don't have any kids anyway so it doesn't matter. And you?"

"Well, I'm not a father either, but it was okay. I haven't been feeling well, in fact I just got out of the hospital a few days ago. My father, he's not...well. I called him to wish him a happy Father's Day and he said it was just like any other day to him."

"A real charmer, eh?"

That makes her laugh a little.

"He broke his glasses today, and I remember when I broke mine he asked if I'd sat my fat ass on them. He said, 'You'd better watch it. You take after your mother's side of the family. They're all fat.'"

There's no clever response to make to that.

"I realize I wasn't the daughter that he could take around and show off. I got scoliosis, I'm only four-feet-four, I got all kinds of health problems. I just wanna make him proud for once, so I'd rather be sick and throw up every other day than be a 350 pound sow, y'know?"

I have nothing I can tell her. We pull up to her address, on the northern edge of Andersonville.

"God, you're so nice, and here I've spilled my guts all out to you," she says.

A man in a yellow T-shirt stands waiting in her doorway. He comes up and pays for the taxi. He's got just the right amount without even asking. I wish her a good night, then make a U-turn and head south on Clark.

ST. PATRICK'S DAY

Driving my first fare of the day, a sweating man crosses our path on Ashland Avenue. His eyes are glassy, unseeing, as he stumbles past. Four or five necklaces of green plastic beads cover his wrongly-buttoned shirt and his fly's all the way down. It's 2:39 p.m.

Three girls, all in green, try to put one of those plastic leprechaun hats on my head as I'm taking them from Wicker Park to Lincoln Park. I ask whether they'd prefer to walk the rest of the way and the hat disappears. Then I tell them I've never celebrated Saint Patrick's Day, which makes them very quiet. They don't get that at all.

At a bus stop on Western Avenue a mohawked, shirtless man is doing a sloppy striptease for no one's benefit in particular. He's just about danced out of his pants by the time I lose sight of him.

I pick up a man and three teenagers from Japonais (an upscale sushi joint). As we pull away, the kids shout, "WE HATE PIGS!" at the cop car parked out front. They're headed to the Drake Hotel and all along the way the man—the father of one of the boys, I presume—points out women walking by. "Did you get a load of *that*, boys?" he keeps asking.

A girl on Fullerton hurls so hard she loses her shoe and bangs her head into the side of a parked car.

A couple and their big galoot of a pal get in on Ashland in Ukrainian Village. They want to go to the Pink Monkey, but first we need to retrace their steps so the big guy can find the credit card he left at one of the last couple bars they visited. The oaf sits up front and asks if I have any Widespread Panic. I say I don't even know their music, which floors him. Apparently that's his preferred soundtrack for a trip to the strip club. He hops out at Chicago and Damen to look for his card and after he's crossed and re-crossed the street a couple times, the girl loses it and yells, "If you don't get back in here we're going to the titty bar without you!" After he finally returns the rest of the ride is spent debating where to stop for a bottle of booze to take in with them. The Pink Monkey's BYOB. On arrival the big man asks if I've got a card so they can call me to pick them up after. I tell him I'm done for the night.

After they've gotten out of the cab a man announces to his wife, "I've gotta hump this cab one time tonight," then proceeds to do just that, rubbing himself against left rear corner of my Scion. Hope she didn't marry him for his sense of humor.

I learn from my passengers' conversation that Groupon employees get bright green jumpsuits monogrammed with their names or a nickname of their choosing. It must be Saint Patrick's Day year-round there.

In Lincoln Square I pick up a guy who turns out to be a sound man in one of the local taverns. I ask him how his night went. "You're playing Television in the cab," he answers, "this is the best part of my night." He wants to know about my night and I tell him it's been a long one. He wants to hear a "crazy" story but I just repeat that it's been a long night.

Toward the end of my shift—about 4:30 a.m.—I'm leaving the Clark gas station at Diversey and Damen when another cab turns in and stops by the car vacuums. The driver gets out and throws all the doors open to air it out. He wasn't as fortunate as I was that year; the pukers got him.

5. SUSPENSION

t the start of September 2010, I receive a letter from the Secretary of State. A cab driver is rarely surprised to get one. The envelope usually contains unsupported charges of moving violations or other false infractions. A parking citation for stopping to unload passengers in front of the Water Tower, for instance—that one took me a good two years to finally make go away. Taxis are a reliable source of revenue for the city. We're out on the streets 24/7, so it's like shooting fish in a barrel. All it takes is showing up for a hearing and the fines usually disappear into thin air. The calculation is that most will not bother to fight it and will just pay up. This letter is different. The header reads: "Notice/Order of Suspension."

There are two speeding tickets listed from last September, one in Ohio and one in New Jersey, as well as a second in Ohio in July. I had forgotten about the ones in September—both received coming back from visiting family in Boston—speeding down late-night turnpikes, trying to get back to Chicago. Three moving violations in 12 months means I'm looking at a nine-month suspension of my license, to begin toward the end of October. September is the month every year that I renew my chauffeur's license. This letter could very well stop me from making a living.

In seven years of driving a taxi in Chicago, I had only gotten two moving violations in one year a couple times. The consequences were to spend some four to six hours in a windowless room getting a refresher course in the rules of the road. This is a whole other thing and I'm at a loss as to what to do. There's now a pain in the pit of my stomach. The next morning, I go to the Yellow Cab offices to seek advice. The man I speak with doesn't have much, except to rifle through a neighboring desk to find a traffic lawyer's business card and to wish me the best of luck.

CHICAGO

The lawyer listed on the card seems nice enough. He's very curious about how I was referred to him and is exceedingly thankful. He must have left his cards at the cab company's offices years ago and forgotten about them. He listens to my problem and advises me to contact the courts in Ohio or New Jersey to have one of the tickets vacated. This means that the cases would be reopened and thus be removed from my driving record. After digging through a drawer overflowing with receipts and paperwork from the last year, I miraculously find the money order used to pay off the Ohio ticket in July. The ticket number is even written out in the memo line. A call to the Bryan County Courthouse in Ohio is less successful however. An elderly woman answers after a few rings—sounding as if I'd troubled her at home—and tells me there's nothing to be done, that basically I should have thought of this at the time of the ticket, and hangs up on me.

The lawyer is incredulous yet his only other idea is to call the court in New Jersey. He insists that this is the only way out of my predicament. I thank him for his advice and set about to find another lawyer. Through friends, I'm referred to an experienced Chicago attorney. He echoes the need to have one of the tickets vacated by reopening the case, but gives me the number of a lawyer in Ohio who might get further than I did on my own.

OHIO

The next few days are spent calling, emailing, and sending various documents to the Ohio lawyer. He's confident that he can get my case reopened, so the knot in my stomach loosens a bit. He never seems to be in his office at the time I call, but the receptionist patches me through to voicemail and he usually calls back by the next day. Everything is moving ahead until I wake one morning to a voicemail from him saying that there's nothing to be done. The judge that he'd be dealing with has a strict policy of not revisiting such cases. He offers to file the motion anyways but makes clear that it would be futile. This ticket cost me $125 already, but the state of Ohio is bent on making me pay more. I thank him for his efforts, swallow hard, and email the Chicago lawyer again.

He suggests a lawyer in New Jersey, saying that if this also goes nowhere, we can apply for a limited license. This would allow me to drive a taxi to earn my living but no other vehicle for the duration of the nine-month suspension. It sounds like a last resort.

NEW JERSEY

The New Jersey lawyer talks like one of those ambulance chasers who advertise on local TV. After hearing me out, he goes on at length about what great relationships he has with the local courts and prosecutors and about how hard he'd work for me. The first order of business is determining the town in which the speeding ticket occurred. It's been a year since the fact, so I'm not sure. I had missed my exit to head west to Chicago, and was instead going south down the New Jersey Turnpike toward Philadelphia. I was upset about being lost so the trooper sitting in the median escaped notice until it was too late. I guessed that it was about an hour north of Philadelphia. The lawyer says that it has to be South Brunswick.

We're in luck because he has a very good working relationship with Judy, the court administrator in South Brunswick. It will be days, however, until he can manage an audience with her. In the meantime, a deluge of phone calls and email rains down from the east. Some are about the long days he works, others are requests for information—such as the ticket number—which he has already gotten from me. Occasionally there are lectures about the justice system and having patience.

I explained in our first conversation about my time constraints—that if this issue isn't addressed by October 1st, I could well be out of a job. He tells me not to worry, that it will all be taken care of. I authorize his $1500 fee on my credit card without a question in the hope that it might motivate him a bit.

By the time he finally manages to put the case back on the calendar in South Brunswick, there are only a few days left in the month. He has me sign and fax back an affidavit, then calls and insists that I get it notarized and shipped overnight to him. Perhaps, I hope, there might finally be some light at the end of this tunnel.

He tells me the next day that the ticket wasn't issued in South Brunswick after all. He tries to imply that the ticket number I gave him was incomplete and that an hour north of Philadelphia has to be South Brunswick; in other words, that it's my fault that he can't figure out how to take care of a simple speeding ticket. What clues him in is that after working on the matter for some two weeks, he finally looks up the infraction on the DMV computer and, what do you know, the citation was issued in Mount Laurel. There's some very good news though, because the prosecutor there is a close personal friend and has been very helpful in the past. He will undoubtedly cooperate with us.

Throughout my three weeks of communication with the New Jersey lawyer, I try a variety of approaches to relay my concerns and the very real urgency of my predicament. Cajoling, scolding, pleading, and out-and-out ranting are all attempted to little effect. In turn, he acts pitiful one moment and short-tempered the next. The stream of inane, nonsequitur missives continues unabated. Sometimes he writes just to say hello or that he'll be in the office late. I stop answering the phone, preferring to have a cooling-off period and answer him only by email or text. Mornings find the inbox clogged with instructions— he wants me to call his assistant to tell him to call the courthouse or write an affidavit or some other such task. It appears that I'm now in the man's employ and not the other way around. When asked why it is my job to relay information from him to his employees no answer is forthcoming.

CHICAGO

September 30th comes and I prepare to go to the Office of Consumer Affairs on Ogden Avenue to plead for an extension for the renewal of my chauffeur's license. Perhaps if I have another week a miracle might happen and the New Jersey ticket might just disappear.

Nearing the top of the line to sign in, my breath quickens, preparing to hear the worst. I tally up my scant savings in my head for about the 150th time since this ordeal began, wondering how long I could to hold out without work. To my utter amazement, the secretary tells me that there's a week's grace period to renew. I turn and run out of there, feeling like my execution has been stayed.

I was advised by the Chicago lawyer that in order to lift the suspension order, I'd need to present the Secretary of State with some record from New Jersey that my case was reopened. My New Jersey lawyer takes this to mean a letter from him, as an officer of the court, testifying to the fact that the prosecutor has agreed to vacate the conviction. When I show up at the Secretary of State's office with this letter, I sign in at the desk, take a number, and wait along with the other penitents. An electronicboard announces the number being served, then one or another of us disappear into the warren of cubicles to hear our fate. When my turn comes I'm confronted with a down-at-the mouth ill-shaven old man who barely glances at the document I'd brought him before announcing that nothing less than a court transcript would be adequate to lift the suspension.

I leave without a word, then punch a door on the way out of the building. This doesn't remedy the situation, but does get my mind off it for a few minutes. When apprised of this latest failure, the New Jersey lawyer doesn't acknowledge the least bit of responsibility. He's much more excited about the fact that his good friend, the prosecutor of Mount Laurel, New Jersey, is willing to let me plead to whatever statute I want, other than speeding, and he'll enter it into the court record. Needless to say, it's my job to research relevant statutes and get back to him as soon as possible. $1500 apparently only buys self-service type legal counsel these days.

My cab company will no longer rent a vehicle to me until my license is updated, so I'm at the mercy of the legal apparatus in the State of New Jersey. Mount Laurel court is only in session Tuesdays and Wednesdays, if my attorney is to be believed. I haven't received any kind of moving violation as a cab driver in over two years, yet because of rushing through a couple one-horse towns, my job is in peril. Paying the exorbitant fines isn't enough. Maybe this is just proof that I'm better off not ever leaving town. I return to the Office of Consumer Affairs (re-christened the

Department of Business Affairs and Consumer Protection and sporting a complete makeover; I barely recognize the place), to see what it would take to save my chauffeur's license. They give me a temporary extension until October 24th to take care of my troubles with the Secretary of State. The New Jersey attorney assures me that my ticket there will be dismissed well before then.

SUSPENDED

I should've known better than to be hopeful.

Foolishly, I believed that—given that he's had six weeks to work at it—my New Jersey lawyer might get somewhere after all. He manages to get a hearing scheduled for 8:30 a.m., October 20th. I wait all morning and into the afternoon for some word from him. Nothing. I finally send an email that simply says, "?" to which the eventual reply is a typically garbled, badly-punctuated ramble about the prosecutor not showing up and that he, the attorney, is still at court. Sometime late in the afternoon he sends a jubilant note, saying that the judge is being very understanding and has agreed to sign a court order stating that my conviction is vacated and the case is back on the court's active calendar. My Perry Mason is charged with drafting this document and getting it to the judge to sign.

The next two days are an endless stream of correspondence between myself, the lawyer, and his young assistant (the one that doesn't acknowledge or respond to email sent to him while he's not physically at the law office). Sometime late on Thursday afternoon comes news that the order has been signed. How would they transport this piece of paper from there to here? It turns into a grind, just like every other step of this excruciating process. Have they faxed it, mailed it, scanned and emailed it? No way to really know. The attorney claims to have an emailed attachment, but can't figure out a way to forward it to me. He also claims to be on an airline flight all Thursday night without access to the internet. He communicates this via email. The assistant, meanwhile, sits waiting in the office for a fax from the judge to appear. No one has any way to check on the status of this elusive note.

Friday morning—the last business day before my suspension was to begin—comes and there is no more mention of the attorney's scanned copy, instead he directs me to contact the assistant, who would fax me the document once it comes in. Around 1:00 p.m., a poorly-composed page, bearing the Mount Laurel judge's supposed signature, arrives. I head downtown to the Secretary of State's office.

Half-an-hour's wait in that airless room and I'm directed to a cubicle to present documents to get the order of suspension lifted. The man behind the desk scrutinizes the sad sheet I present him, noting the crossed-out line near the bottom, and says what I fear: they can only accept an official document of the New Jersey court. No copy or fax would do. There's nothing more he can do for me.

Going back out into the Friday afternoon crowd on State Street, I try to get my breathing back under control. No doors are harmed this time; instead I write to Clarence Darrow to apprise him of the news. His swift response consists of claiming that I'd never told him that an original of the document was required. As on other occasions in our acquaintance, it appears that it's on me to know the intricacies of law and bureaucracy; not on the man paid and, allegedly, trained to do so. A few more messages back and forth followed, culminate in this:

NOTHING YOU HAVE DONE HAS HELPED ME.

If you couldn't figure out that the Secretary of State of Illinois wouldn't accept that garbled note (with lines crossed out!) as an official document, then I don't know what else to say to you. The bottom line is that that speeding ticket is still on my record and my driver's license will be suspended for nine months on October 24th.

What this means is we're at the same place we were six weeks ago when I made the mistake of calling you.

Talking to you on the phone only raises my blood pressure further because most of what you say is either irrelevant to the subject at hand or just plain incomprehensible.

I'm just about done dealing with you.

Not a peep from him since. I contact the Chicago attorney to get me a hardship hearing with the Secretary of State to try to get a limited license that would allow me to drive a cab only, for the duration of the suspension.

POSTSCRIPT

Another week passes before my East Coast legal mastermind is able to harness the power of the post office and send the original New Jersey court order which lifts my suspension. The only silver lining to this ludicrous saga is that the $1500 fee I authorized the lawyer to charge my credit card never goes through. It's the one and only instance that his ineptitude works in my favor.

ome rides make a driver happy. A funny fare, a good story, or a kind word might get us through another long shift.

REGULAR ROUTE

An "O" next to a fare displayed on the Gandalf means that it's a time order. More often than not it's a trip to the airport and thus is snapped up seconds after it flickers across the screen. I'd just left the house to start work and, logging into the system, saw "500-1O" appear as the only currently available fare. The cab company divides the city into zones with odd numbers for the South Side and evens for the North. Zone 500 covers much of Bridgeport and south to the edge of where the Union Stockyards used to be. It's within a couple miles of where I live, so I key in the bid and get the call.

It's not an airport job. Instead, the screen displays an address on 38th Street, followed by: "Mon-Thur: 3:00 p.m., Fri: 12:30 p.m. // Please call with Cab#." It all comes back to me. I hadn't driven him for several years, not since Checker was its own company and hadn't yet been taken over by Yellow Cab. There seemed to be a lot more regular riders then. I spent most afternoons ferrying disabled kids home as part of the Mobility Program. To supplement RTA handicapped vans, the city contracted cab companies to pick up developmentally disabled teenagers and adults. When Checker went under and was swallowed up by Yellow, a lot of that business went away. Perhaps it was just coincidence or a change in city policy. Mr. Hall wasn't a Mobility ride, but he reminded me of that time.

I pull up to the low building that houses Midwest Lighting on 38th Street, a couple blocks west of Halsted, right at 3:00 p.m. It's a nondescript structure painted baby blue. Workers soon start to spill out, many pausing to light Salems, Marlboros, or Kools before walking away. Mr. Hall comes out a few minutes later. He's a lot more bent over than I remember him, but what he says is just as it always was: "All right. We're going to Ogilvie Train Station, but there's a particular way that we need to take."

I have no doubt that he instructs every driver, every one of the five days a week that he takes this trip, in exactly this same way. "We're going to go to the end of this block, then turn left on Halsted, then take your very first right." He waits until I've accomplished this before resuming. "Now, we'll keep going straight for four blocks until we get to Wallace, then we stay on that until 29th Street." I'm not sure why I find him dictating the route endearing; there's an assumption in it that the driver doesn't know the best way to get to his destination. I've been guilty in the past of taking quiet pleasure in getting stuck in gridlock because of a passenger's insistence on a particular route I knew to be wrong. Mr. Hall isn't wrong. How long has he been retracing this route? Thirty, forty years would be my best guess.

"At 29th Street you turn right and go down to the second stop sign, that'll be Canal. Turn left. There will be two speed bumps coming up very quickly, one after the other. We go straight all the way to Madison Street now." He's quiet until we pass 18th, then advises, "There's train tracks that are pretty ripped up just past this rise, so I'd slow down... The rest is up to you."

We take the final left turn from Canal onto Madison and stop in front of the station entrance. The meter reads $11.25 (plus a dollar extra for the gas surcharge). He takes out a baggie full of coins, holds it up to the light, and fishes out a quarter, then wraps a ten and three singles around it and hands itto me. "I thank you again," he says before leaving.

There's a certain comfort in being part of the old man's routine.

MOOD DIRECTOR

I answer a call in Humboldt Park. It's one of those new-construction condo buildings. The ones with the fake-brick façade the wrong shade of red and cheap cinderblock the rest of the way back to the alley. A young, well-dressed man comes out hauling two oversized vinyl bags. I open the hatch to load his cargo and he says, "Don't worry, it's a mascot costume."

I take him to a nightclub just off the Ohio feeder in River North. The fare is about ten dollars and he asks for eight, then seven dollars change from his twenty.

"Do I hear six?" I deadpan, making him laugh.

Two weeks later, a radio call brings me back to the cinderblock condo in Humboldt. The guy recognizes me right away, "You got a card? It's a real bitch getting a cab around here." I tell him I don't. He gives me his though. It has his name and *Mood Director* underneath.

"Remember that mascot costume? It's a bear suit. In the place I work at, there are go-go dancers up behind the bar and they're getting sprayed with water, like they're taking a shower. The guys eat that shit up. I sneak up behind the ladies, in full costume, and pretend to be doing 'em,—'Uh, uh, uh,'—you know, it's my job to make sure everyone's having a good time. Thinking next I'm gonna be a gorilla and I'll get one of the other guys to dress like a giant banana and I'll chase him all over the club. Awesome, right? We have pillow fights, all sorts of crazy shit. I do one of these stunts and you should see all the cameras come out, flashes all over the place, click, click, click!"

I pull over in front of the club. He even remembers the bit about "Do I hear six?" from last time.

All the while he's selling, inviting me to stop in, to ask for him by name. I thank him and give back his seven dollars change.

BOURBON GIRL

At a red on Fullerton, I look over to see the peroxide-blond girl, who'd been walking a dog with a grubby, tattooed guy, run over my way. "Can you take us?" she asks uncertainly. When I nod, she turns back and motions the guy with the dog over. She climbs in and coaxes the cowering pit bull up onto the back seat; the guy's last in, shutting the door behind him.

"I just rescued her from some bangers down the street," he announces with some pride. I look back at him and see face tattoos and piercings, a couple scabbed-over cuts and bruises, and a goofy grin. A crusty punk. The girl is a bit less thrilled with it all.

"You're not bringing another damn stray home, I swear to God! I'll put you out. It's too damn much," she threatens. He tries to placate her, pointing out what a good dog this is. The pit just stands up on the seat and accepts his love quietly, poking that brick of a head between the seats every now and then. She does seem like a sweet dog. The girl doesn't stand a chance.

"Look at how her ears are clipped all the way back. They do that for when they fight 'em. There's a big vein that runs through their ears and they can bleed out if they get bitten. Her leg's all fucked up too. What kind of person sells his dog for $25?" he asks me, though of course it's meant to bolster the case to his lady.

"One that doesn't care about the dog very much," I answer. It's hard not to take his side.

"Do what you have to. I'll sleep with her by the underpass if I have to," he continues, feeling more confident by the second. Just then, we stop at a light and see some guys waiting at a bus stop. One of them recognizes me and waves but the kid thinks the guy's waving to him. He rolls down the window and holds the dog up for them to see. The guys all laugh and wave back, playing along, humoring another crazy cab passenger. They've probably seen it a million times. The light changes and we roll on.

"We have two in the house already. Where are we gonna put her?" the girl protests quietly. She knows she's already lost. He's christened the dog Bourbon Girl and keeps using the name like it's been hers for years. The punk and the pit jump out at Wilson and Kedzie and wait at the curb while the girl pays for the cab.

"Thank you so much for taking us. Most cabbies don't like dogs. We really appreciate it," she tells me wearily, handing me seven dollars over their ten dollar fare and crawling out. As I drive away I see her squat down and pet Bourbon Girl's head.

CHARLES BRONSON

I'm in the 7-Eleven at Wrightwood and Lincoln buying a snack when two young guys approach me. One has a baby face with puffy cheeks and curly hair, the other's scruffier, attempting some sort of facial hair. They're both buying blunts.

"That you?" the scruffy one asks, pointing at the cab parked out front.

"Know where LaSalle Power Company is?" they want to know. Yes,

I know where it is. It's one of a couple dozen gigantic, indistinguishable bars in River North; at one time, the location housed Michael Jordan's restaurant.

"How long will it take? We're not from around here. We're from Notre Dame. By the way, what do you think of Charles Bronson?"

Being asked by a 20-year-old about the star of *Death Wish* kind of throws me. I tell him that I think Bronson's pretty cool.

"You see, I think Charles Bronson is pretty much the greatest. When I was little, my dad used to always say, 'Don't mess with Charles Bronson,' so I had to find out who he was. Now I own like thirty of his movies. Did you know that Charles Bronson lost his virginity at age five-and-a-half? That's according to Charles Bronson and I wouldn't dare to question him. He called it 'making it.'"

Not to be outdone, his friend tells me about the term paper he wrote for his World War ll film class. He favored *The Great Escape* and *The Dirty Dozen* over *Bataan* because the latter did not feature Bronson. "Charles Bronson smoked cigarettes when he was six. He only died in one movie, *The Mechanic*, and that was just so he could prove that he could still kill from beyond the grave. Pow!"

This is like attending a graduate-level seminar. They're very devoted. Only once during the ride does the conversation stray from Bronson and that's a brief tangent on what disagreements have caused them to get into fist fights. "I punched a kid in the face because he said Creed was lame. Because they're not. They're awesome," the curly one says.

"I chipped this dude's tooth cuz he accused me of having Nickelback on my iPod," his buddy counters.

Outside the LaSalle Power Company we're one of half a dozen other taxis, limos, and valeted vehicles clogging up the block.

"When was the last time you saw a Charles Bronson film and what's your favorite, sir?" the curly one wants to know. I'm not sure how to answer. "May I suggest *Death Wish 4: The Crackdown*? It's a particular favorite of mine," he offers.

I thank him for the tip and watch as they get out of the cab and make their way to the back of the velvet-roped line waiting to get into the bar.

It's heartening to know that the younger generation hasn't forgotten about the heroes of the past.

HER BIRTHDAY

A large woman waits for me to get to the head of the line at the Midway Airport taxi stand. She's glad to see my Scion. "After being jammed into that airplane seat, last thing I want is to be in the back of one of them cop cars." I move the passenger seat all the way up but it's still a tight fit. She exhales and asks to go to 45th and Woodlawn.

"So where's this weather that made my plane four hours late?" she asks. I tell her it was really coming down earlier. She's unhappy because it's her birthday and the delay has made her have to cancel her dinner reservation. "How am I gonna get my $75 lobster tail now?" We're going east on Garfield and she pulls out her phone, puts it on speaker, and dials to check her messages. A succession of voices wish her a happy birthday, many make her laugh, a few make me laugh as well. Calling one back, she speaks into the phone like it's a mic, "Thank you, Lumpy Earl, you're the first one who sang for me!" After she's done she explains that he's an uncle who'd been dropped on his head as a child, leaving lumps in his head, and that the nickname has stuck. "A 45-year-old man named Lumpy, yup."

The next message she checks makes her even happier, "Oooooh, Ernesto's back. I got some work for him!" She explains that Ernesto had decorated most of her house but left to take a full-time job. "People come over my place and see the Venetian marble and think it's for real, but I tell them, 'No, it's just painted.' They can't believe it. The man is so good. Took me about five years to save up to pay him to do all the rooms in my place. He's a perfectionist too. All my neighbors are so jealous."

"See," I point out, "it's not such a bad birthday after all." She doesn't disagree.

She tells me how hard it is for a woman to get work done around the house and not get ripped off. "What they don't know is that I work with contractors all the time," she says. "I know what things cost. Just the other week we were having the bathrooms redone at the office. It was a million-dollar job and they didn't wanna put full-length mirrors in the ladies' room. I took it all the way to the top. Us women need to be able to look at ourselves. You'd think it was all single men making these decisions. It pays to complain. It's how things get done."

She looks out the window at the men hanging around outside a liquor store and shakes her head.

"It's been a tough one this year, though. My mother passed on a few months back. It was just shy of my folks' 50th anniversary too, so that five grand I'd been saving up to throw them a bash went for the funeral instead. It's not the same not getting that call from her at 6:22 a.m., telling me that was the time I was born. Guess it was just her time."

We cut north through Washington Park to 51st. A couple blocks east, we pass the hulking black SUV permanently installed to guard President Obama's home. "He sure makes it tough on us when he comes back here with the security and all," she comments. "I met him back when he was a senator and he was real down to earth, called me back personally one time when I had a complaint too. A few years back a friend said she was having a fundraiser for him and I ask, 'For what? He already a senator.' I couldn't believe it. Thought they'd kill him for sure. He ain't done nothin' for me personally except freeze my pay. I work for the government. B's a good man though, I'll stick with him."

It's $21.45 on the meter—plus a $2 airport charge and a $1 gas surcharge—when we stop in front of her house. "Huh. A lot cheaper coming back than going to the airport. Guy took me up Lake Shore. It was quick but, dang." I explain that taking Lake Shore Drive from her house to Midway actually adds several miles and more than a few dollars to the trip. I wish her a happy birthday and watch as she crosses the street toward the gate of a townhouse on Woodlawn. It's one in a row of identical others, but it's hers.

KIDS

On Damen Avenue in Bucktown, a bug-eyed old hack leans out of his taxi and jabs his finger toward Armitage, barking that there's a lady and two kids needing a cab around the corner. Sure enough, there they are at the corner of Wolcott, three pairs of hands waving wildly in all directions. A curly-haired girl, followed by a boy, maybe a year younger, with mom bringing up the rear. "Thank you for stopping for us," she says, settling in. "Can you take us to the Sheraton downtown? It's on St. Clair, I think."

"North Water," I correct her, getting on the Kennedy inbound.

The little girl is the talkative one. "Why did all those taxis drive by us and they didn't stop?" she wants to know. I suggest that maybe they had passengers or were on their way to pick someone up. She says there were lots of empty ones and doesn't seem satisfied with my explanation at all. "This taxi is all new. Did you buy it?"

Mom wonders aloud whether it's because the other cabs don't want to put up with all the questions. "Bet you didn't know what you were letting yourself in for, eh?"

The whole Chicago skyline is before us as we inch east through afternoon traffic. "My daddy works in the Serious Tower," the boy announces. "Can we take taxis all day, Mommy?"

She explains to him that Daddy has the car with him at the hotel, which disappoints him. "Do you want to eat hot dogs again for dinner?" she asks him. The woman's pretty worn down by the kids, so, seeing that they're occupied with the taxi and its driver, she gets on her phone and turns away to look out the window.

"How old are you? Are you 45?" the girl asks.

"Forty," I answer.

"My daddy's 43 and you look older than him. How come is that?" Getting no response, she turns to her mother and asks, "Is Mexico where aliens go? I don't like aliens."

The woman keeps talking on the phone, paying the girl no mind.

"I like aliens. There was an alien outside my window one time. He had a driver's license. I don't know how he got it because he's too small," the boy volunteers.

Coming back to me, the girl says, "Do you have nightmares about E.T.? Because I do."

I tell her I don't.

The boy adds, "Do you like aliens?"

"I've never met one," I answer.

We stop in the Sheraton's driveway and the kids' attention shifts to the doorman with his whistle, cap, and coat with epaulets, holding the door open for them. Mom thanks me but the kids are long gone without a goodbye. On to the next thing.

GARRETT'S POPCORN

A girl with close-cropped hair walks up and asks if I'm available. I'm at the corner of 21st and State, checking my email after dropping off a fare at Reggie's rock club. I nod and she asks me to wait for the rest of her friends to show up. Three guys and one more girl arrive carrying balloons and small bags of Garrett's popcorn. They're all dressed like they'd been at prom—an off-kilter adult prom. They pile in, balloons and all, asking to go to Berlin, a club on the north side.

They talk about what people wore. There's a lot of teasing and laughter, all of which fogs up the cab's windows as we speed up Lake Shore Drive on this chilly night. A high-pitched male voice from the back announces that the two girls are moving in together. "How long have you two been together, a couple weeks?"

"Eight months," one of the girls answers, mock-defensively.

"Have you heard this one: What does a lesbian bring on a first date? A toothbrush."

Everyone in the cab roars.

"What does a she bring on a second date? A U-Haul! You can't be mad at me either. I heard that from a lesbian!"

They discuss how long it's appropriate to date before moving in together. The consensus seems to be that eight months is too soon.

"Of course everyone in this cab's gay so maybe it's different in the straight world?" one wonders aloud. A moment later they're asking for my take. I ponder it a moment then agree that eight months is probably a bit too soon. A cheer goes up from the back seat.

All this time the pudgy kid sitting in the front seat hasn't said much. He's dressed in a blue blazer that looks like it might belong to his dad and has spent much of the ride either stuffing popcorn into his face or napping. A voice from the back asks him, "Gustavo, how you doing, girl?"

Gustavo wakes up and mumbles something back.

"Didn't know you did drag, girl!"

"You haven't heard of Mel-ahnie Ninja?" Gustavo answers haughtily.

From more of their conversation it's clear that except for the girls these aren't close friends but rather acquaintances. They've seen each other at the clubs. As we pass Spin one comments, "I think Spin isn't dreadful anymore like it used to be."

One of the girls disagrees, sounding almost horror stricken. At Berlin it turns out that only a couple of them are getting out. Seems that the girls have to judge a fashion contest at another club down the street and one of the boys has work in the morning. A couple of the boys pull all the balloons out of the cab and tidy up the back seat, apologizing for the mess. Gustavo hands me a bag of Garrett's as he gets out, leaving caramel-and cheese-covered popcorn all over the seat.

I drop the girls at a place further west on Belmont then head toward Uptown. I ask my remaining passenger what event they were all at. He says it's called the Wonka Ball, and it is indeed a sort of prom to benefit gay kids. He's dressed in a burgundy-colored velvet jacket and ruffled shirt in a pattern I'd have trouble describing. He wouldn't be out of place in Wonka's Chocolate Factory at all, though. He tells me he does graphic design for the event, then asks how long I've been with my girlfriend. He congratulates me and wishes me luck after hearing we've just moved in together.

His place is on Magnolia, just in back of the Uptown Theater. I drive off, getting to the bottom of that bag of Garrett's before making it much more than a mile or two.

MAINTENANCE MAN

He gets in at the bus stop at Chicago and Western. "Can't wait for that bus no more. Gotta get to work," he says, giving a Lincoln Park address, smelling strongly of beer.

He tells me it's only his second day back on the job. He was in an accident that shattered his hand.

"It was at Cortland and Ashland. You know that corner?" he asks.

"Yeah, it's a nightmare," I say.

"You know how the lanes split up and there are columns in between? This guy makes a turn right after and smashes right into me. I had a '96 Saturn. It was totaled. He was driving an SUV with Florida plates so maybe that's why he didn't know he wasn't supposed to turn there. It's one of the first intersections with a red-light camera in the city. Did you know that?"

Just as he's saying this we pass Fullerton and Ashland and see the tell-tale flash as a camera catches a car for crossing on the red. He claps his hands and cheers.

"Anyways, his insurance was good and covered everything but after a while you go sorta crazy not doing anything in your house, y'know? I've never missed more than a couple days of work and I've been working there fifteen years. They give me all these painkillers, Vicodin, but they don't help me at all. I'd rather let Mother Nature heal me. I guess I could sell those pills but I'd get in trouble—heh-heh-heh. I'm just kidding, I wouldn't do that. Beer's good enough for me. You know Warsteiner? Good German beer. I'm just glad to be back workin'."

"What do you do?"

"I work maintenance at this high-rise you're taking me to. It's right next to that new one they're building. I work midnights, 11:30 p.m. to 8:00 a.m. I just got back so I'm not as fast as I used to be. I gotta wax and buff 42 floors every night. I work by myself."

He tells me he's lived in the neighborhood where I picked him up all his life. "I live on Rice, you know they cut off the end of the block—made it into a cul-de-sac—but it used to go through and there was a drug house on that corner. They cleaned it up. Me and my sister own it, otherwise there's no way I could live there. I don't have a million bucks, heh-heh-heh."

We pull into the circle drive of his building but he tells me to stop short of the glass doors because he has to go in through the back. He pays, saying to keep the two dollars change, and walks away.

OLDIES

The two girls were laughing before they even get in the cab. They're at the corner of Division and Western and want to go to Belmont and Clark. Neither one can be too far into her 20s. "Ridiculous. Whenever you and I get together it's like this," one says to the other, barely able to keep a straight face. "That's why we belong together," the other answers.

They tell me they're running late for the Cars concert at the Riviera. "Belmont and Clark's not where the Riv is," I remark.

"Yeah, we forgot the tickets at home," one of them answers. I tell them they're about 25 years too late for the Cars. The art of fading away has been long forgotten these days. Every band gets back together now and if you weren't around the first time it's understandable that you'd want to hear those songs you've loved since you were little, coming out of the mouths of the people that wrote them, while you jump up and down, reliving a past you were never part of.

"We went to the Devo show at the Vic last year and we were totally the youngest ones there."

"I hope there's some old guys there who want to buy us everything!"

I assure them that there would be no shortage of those. One of the reasons I can't go to too many of these nostalgia shows is those old guys. Unlike these girls, they were there the first time and apparently left something there that they've been trying to retrieve ever since. It's that high school reunion business and you can find it at concert halls in any town, most any day of the week now.

"What else are we supposed to do on a Wednesday night?"

"So you're really into that '80s music, eh?" I ask.

"Of course! Night Ranger, Toto, that shit's the best," was the giggling answer from the back.

"It's because you weren't alive during that decade that you like it," I offer.

"So, like, it wasn't the cool people that liked the Cars in the '80s, it was the dorks, right?" one wants to know.

I can't even remember.

They start talking about what they'd be doing if it was the '80s now. "We'd be wearing business suits and doing blow right now!"

"I'd totally be doing that one-armed drummer from Def Leppard!" They're scream-laughing now.

"Okay, so here's the plan: run up and get the tickets, throw some paint on my face, roll a spliff or two, and smoke it on the way to the show. Cool?"

"Man, I hope Toto's opening for The Cars."

We're about a block from Belmont and Clark now. I ask where they want to be dropped off, and they say their place is right above the L & L Tavern. "It's a really cool place, by the way," one says helpfully. I know it's a cool bar, having gone there for the first time some 20 years ago.

"Keep listening to rock-'n-roll, sir," one says, as they bounce out.

I promise them that I will.

ometimes a passenger will make a driver wish he'd never gone out to work. Ugly, venal, and racist boors wander about the city's streets day and night. Every cab driver draws a lousy hand now and then. The only good thing is that unlike a waiter or bartender stuck with a shitty customer, we're rid of them in minutes rather than hours.

GOD'S GIFT

He has an unlit half-cigarette between his teeth as he gets in on Elston, across from the Abbey Pub. "I turned the cigarette off, don't worry," he assures me. "Take me to Division and Pulaski, or somewhere close to there. I'll tell you. Normally, I pay like $17, but if it gets to be ridiculous, I'll just get out. I'm not makin' much money."

Then he notices the touch screen playing ads, not two feet from his face. "What's with all the technology in this cab?" he asks. "I used to drive a cab like ten years ago and there was nuthin', just black girls in the back. Hahahaha."

"What are you, an American?" he wants to know. When I tell him I'm not from here, he takes a moment to ponder, then asks, "Wait. You're white; not like one of those Arabians. I started with American United, you know that? This must be your own cab 'cuz there's no shield."

"No," I answer, "these new cabs don't have shields and shields won't protect you anyway."

He doesn't agree. "You shittin' me? A nigger tried to rob me with a coathanger, I slam on the brakes and *BASH!* his fuckin' head goes into the shield. Nigger tried to hold me up with a real gun, same thing—*BASH!* right into the shield. I'm 23 years old, I ain't puttin' up with that shit.

"I'm on my way to see my black girlfriend, but I might stop and see my white girlfriend on the way, maybe. She's gettin' old though, her pussy ain't what it used to be. The black one's cool, I'll go see her. Got a 22-year-old one too; she's straight-up crazy. Don't like the Spanish chicks, I just wind up beating them up." We're going south on Pulaski now, passing Armitage, and he starts complaining about the touch screen again. "I can't stand it talkin' to me like this." When I suggest he look out the window instead, he says he's all about talking to the driver. Just my luck.

"I'm Polish and Austrian and Irish, I'm all mixed up. My father drove a cab for 18 years, my roommate still does it. I loved it and I used to drive drunk as hell all the time. Got two DUIs. I'd have a beer in my hand, doing 70 up Lincoln. Bitches used to thank me, 'Oh, you got me home so fast. You want to come upstairs?' Fuck yeah, I did."

He's quiet a minute, but as we pass North Avenue, he remarks, "I been gettin' high since I'm 16. Ain't nothin' new there. Your meter's runnin' slow. Some guys, it runs fast, yours is slow, I'm just tellin' ya. I know these things."

I thank him for the information and add that it means he'd win out on the fare if he is right.

"I don't wanna win. I want everybody to win. Except the Chicago police. I don't want them to win, they got too many tickets on me. Get rid of that beard. Better to be clean-shaven; you'll look ten years younger. You'll get all kindsa pussy, trust me, but the beard's no good. Don't wanna look like some goddamn A-rab, do ya?"

We pull up to a liquor store at the corner of Division and Pulaski and he wants me to leave him there. "I'll go in here. The A-rabs, they like me in there. They're my friends... don't pick up no one out here. Nothin' but niggers out here."

The meter reads $10.65 plus the $1 gas surcharge, making his total $11.65. He gives me $12 and goes into the liquor store.

THE RUNT

He's a little unfortunate-looking man. The first time I drove him he got arrested in a Jewel supermarket and I didn't get paid. A couple years later, when his Humboldt Park address came up on the Gandalf, I did a double take but took him anyways. It was obvious he had no memory of our first meeting. He wanted to go to the same Jewel at Roosevelt and Wabash, but this time I made sure he gave me the money before going into the store. He wasn't as out of it as the first time, though he'd drift in and out in a narcotized way, unaware and unconcerned about his appearance or much else. When he returned from the store that time he gave an address about a mile away, then paid up and left without incident.

This time, he takes forever coming out of the house on Evergreen. An old man—who's come out of the house to signal he's on his way before—waves at me to stay. The runt comes down the stairs and climbs into the passenger seat of the van parked in front of the house. The old man has to drag him out of there and point him toward my cab. "63rd and Western," he's able to mutter before passing out. Aside from occasional burbling, mewling sleep sounds, he keeps quiet as we drive south.

Approaching 63rd Street, I turn on the interior light and tell him that we're close and I need a precise address. This has no effect whatsoever, so I pull over, turn around and shout at the top of my lungs for him to wake up. His eyes briefly flutter before rolling back up into his head. A few more hollers produce the news that he has no money, that it's at the house; but what house and where? That isn't so easy to say. He insists he's tired from working all day and just wants to sleep. I ask what he thinks I'm doing here, whether he thinks I'm hauling his sorry ass around town just for the fun of it. He doesn't have an answer—and then he then tries to get out of the taxi. "Aren't you forgetting something?" I ask. "I got no money," he repeats. "Ok, we're going to the police," I say, and suddenly, he remembers his address and produces a twenty and a five as if by magic. Now he's sorry, but he's had his second, third, and fourth chances with me. "DON'T EVER CALL THIS CAB COMPANY AGAIN, SHIT-HEEL!" is what he gets by way of goodbye.

I call the dispatcher to ask her to flag the address, that dealing with this isn't worth whatever money any driver might make, and she says she'll try. I doubt that they'll take a cab driver's word and blackball the runt. No doubt I haven't seen the last of him.

QUIÑONES

On the deserted corner of California and Elston, an older man in a flannel shirt and stocking cap hails me by holding up a plastic cup as if about to give a toast. We go south on California toward Humboldt Park. "Hey, you're white, so I know how to act," he informs me. "Now, my Vietnamese wife don't get it, but I do. I love living in Chicago. Know why? 'Cuz this place is real." He gets on the phone, barking for the guy on the other end to come out and meet us. We idle across from the park, just past North Avenue. A shirtless young man in a second-floor window scurries about throwing on clothes then runs across the icy street to the cab. He wears yellow pajama bottoms and a winter coat.

"We need whiskey," the old man says, so I drive toward Division to find a liquor store. "I don't like the nigger. Know he talks shit about you?" he tells his young friend. "Yeah, he comes in with that fat bitch with the mulatto kid and says you're stealing." He gives the guy his plastic cup for safekeeping while he runs out to the store. I can see him talking to the counter man for quite a while, then when he comes back we have to make another stop to get cigarettes. "I like this guy," he says, "Those Paki drivers, they don't understand what I want. They take me to the police station, can you believe that?"

We're back at the young guy's place. He gives me a twenty and reaches through the partition to shake hands, "Quiñones," he says by way of introduction, as if we'd just met.

AUNTIE

It's 12:30 a.m. on a Wednesday night and there isn't much going on out here. I'm grateful for the radio call in Humboldt Park. I stop by the California Avenue address and wait. A few minutes later a drawn woman of indeterminate age opens the door tentatively, slips outside, then takes her time locking up.

She might be 50, she might be 40, but she's got very few teeth left and a piercing where a mole might be on her cheek.

"47th and Harlem, you know where that's at?" she asks.

"Sure," I answer.

"That's where I'm going. Never been there before. I'm going to meet my nephew at a strip club, can you believe that? Him dragging me out of the house at this hour?"

"Do you have an address for this place?"

"No. Let me call him and get it for you."

I turn the taxi towards the Eisenhower as her cellphone rings and rings. I hear her counting coins back there and this makes me wonder whether I'll be getting paid with laundry quarters for this trek. She finally gets someone on the line as we're exiting at Harlem. She tells them to go get her nephew, "Papi, tell him it's his auntie calling."

She keeps reassuring me that I'll get paid, that if she doesn't have enough her nephew would take care of it. I say I'm not worried. She keeps counting and re-counting her coins. She tells me she has three children ranging in age from 17 to 22.

"My oldest, he dropped out of college after one semester and I still gotta pay for that. I didn't know about it but you could get a—what do you call it? A mother loan or something. It's cool to have kids. Until you get the bill."

At 47th Street there's a gas station on one side and a forest preserve on the other. I ask her to call the nephew again. She passes the phone to me and over crowd noise he keeps repeating and repeating, "My partner, he's got two fifties. What you wanna do?" until the line cuts out. There was something about passing the forest preserve in the pauses around the talk of fifty dollar bills so I take a chance and go west on 47th. After emerging from the woods we pass a vacant-looking garage. In its lot a sedan sits idling, the tail pipe smoking, all the windows fogged up. My passenger is now panicking.

"He knows what I'm like. I have anxiety attacks, I never even taken a cab before. I'm bipolar. WHERE IS HE?"

We cross Joliet Road and see a neon sign ahead: "All Stars." The lot is full of trucks and beat-up older-model vehicles. She pays me the $27 fare in paper bills—not laundry quarters—and runs out, into the arms of a pudgy man with a thin mustache, who's just come out of the building.

The well-dressed man hails me at State and Grand on a Saturday night.

"Can you take me to 1520 North Damen? Take the Kennedy and get off at Division not North, I don't want to get stuck dealing with that. How are you doing?"

"All right. And you?"

"Couldn't be better. I'm wonderful. I'm back in town for a few days and on my way to surprise a few friends. They have no idea I'm here. They're going to be thrilled. What kind of vehicle is this?"

"A Scion."

"Is it the xB or the xD?

"xB, I think."

"I couldn't imagine driving a car without a stick shift. I'm an expert driver and I like to feel that I'm guiding the machine rather than it guiding me."

"Well, you might feel different if you had to do the kind of driving I do. Try driving 80 a week in stop-and-go city traffic and you'll want to make it as easy on yourself as you can. Driving's got nothing to do with pleasure. It's work."

"I love speed. Last year I made it from L.A. to San Antonio in ten hours. TEN HOURS! That's around 1300 miles. I was in New Mexico for all of 47 minutes. That's like a hundred miles. I saw the sun come up somewhere in Texas and I was lucky it had been a cool night or the car would've overheated. I was really pushing it."

I don't respond or comment on his claims. The fact that the man has to boast of his prowess behind the wheel to a complete stranger baffles me. Perhaps the fact that I am a cab driver makes him think his feats might impress me or that we could commiserate over shared interests. Neither is the case but my silence doesn't dampen his enthusiasm.

"I could never get a crotch-rocket. Can you imagine? Going 200-250 mph? I'd break every law."

Trying to get him off the subject of speed, I ask why he'd moved away.

"I had to move to Dallas because of a family situation about seven months ago. It's alright, I mean my apartment costs $550 and it's right in the middle of town, you couldn't do that here, no way. I'm bartending. Making $7-10K a month. You can't beat that. But it's just slinging drinks, it's not the kind of bartending I like to do. I prefer to make quality cocktails." As we near the 1500 block of Damen, he points out the yellowish light over the hidden door of the Violet Hour and says that that is where he is headed to meet his friends, reiterating how thrilled they're going to be to see him. I have no doubt that they will be. He worries over his bills, settling on an amount that includes a tip that is midway between acceptable and insulting, bids me goodnight and strides across the street.

TAX RETURN

It's a frigid Tuesday night and Western Avenue's a ghost town except for a woman in leggings and fake fur desperately waving both arms my way from the bus stop at Augusta. I stop. There's not much to lose on a night like this.

"You don't know how happy I am to see you," she says, "this is crazy-man weather. This is the type of night that if I was homeless, people would have to get sacrificed. I'd be all Jeffrey Dahmer out here to survive. Alright. I'm going to the 2500 block of Monroe. My brother's there and he's got my tax return for me. He got some Jew accountant who got us way more than we deserve. Believe me, I wouldn't be out here if there wasn't money to be made. Don't worry now. I've got money. You'll get paid."

I tell her I'm not worried. It's a short trip so even if she runs it won't be much of a loss. She gets on the phone and says that she'll be there in four minutes. She chatters to me about how the area's in the process of getting gentrified, how most of the projects are gone now. I assume that this is to ease my fears about going there but she seems much more nervous about the whole thing than I am. She counts and recounts the crumpled bills in her hands.

The 2500 block of Monroe is mostly empty lots with a couple of forlorn-looking four-flats here and there to keep it from reverting to the prairie which was once here. We stop in front of one of these. A kid in a puffy jacket stamps his feet and hops around to keep from freezing in place. This must be her tax guy.

I turn off the meter and ask for $5.95 but she says to wait, that she'll be going back in a minute. She runs across the street and, after exchanging a few words with the guy, jumps into the driver's seat of a car parked out front while he gets in on the passenger's side. She's out seconds later and running back toward the taxi. She opens the door, then squats down with her back to me and asks me not to look while she urinates, "Good thing I got a tissue," she mutters before plopping back inside and giving an address on Cortez, a couple blocks from where I'd picked her up. As we pull away the kid across the street looks like he's about to piss himself laughing. "This is the time of night and place to get killed in Chicago," she says.

She gets on the phone again and says to have ten bucks ready for her when she gets there for the cab. It sounds like whomever she's talking to needs a bit of convincing. She hangs up with a deep sigh and complains,

"My husband. He's such a Jew. He's telling me to make sure and get a receipt for the ride. Jesus." We stop and I see a basement apartment light go on. She hands me four bucks, then runs out and reaches through the chain-link fence and grabs a $10 bill from the window and returns with it. The fare is $11.95 and she asks for a dollar back, thanks me and runs back to the house only to turn right back around. She's forgotten her receipt. Gotta keep careful records where taxes are concerned.

POSTAL

A well-dressed woman waves from across Milwaukee Avenue. It's a Saturday afternoon, so the streets of Wicker Park are barely passable and swinging the cab around isn't an option. I look away from her and start considering whether to turn onto Damen or North when the light changes. She crosses through the now-moving traffic and takes her time about getting in, making the motorists behind me convey their displeasure loudly.

"Marina City," she commands.

A hard right puts us east on North Avenue, inching toward the expressway and downtown. "Which way are you going?" she barks out, as if outraged about something.

I explain the fairly standard route I have in mind. "We'll take the Kennedy to the Ohio feeder, then, depending on traffic, one of several southbound streets to Kinzie, go left to State Street, and a right to Marina City."

We're moving at a snail's pace and I can practically feel her frustration like hot breath on the back of my neck. Her tone is brusque enough that I have to point out that a bit of politeness wouldn't hurt. I also wonder whether she's turned around in an unfamiliar neighborhood.

"I'm just asking a question. It's my right to do that," she snaps.

"Perhaps you'd prefer to take another cab," I suggest.

"No. You're going to take me where I say."

"You know you're really rude?" I ask.

"That's just the way I talk. You ain't the first to say that. It's not personal. I work for the Post Office and gotta put up with a lotta foolishness," she answers.

I just start laughing. The tension's broken for a spell as she tells me a bit about her 26-and-a-half years on the job. I ask about all the cuts coming to the postal service but she seems confident her job's safe. We empathize with one another for having to put up with idiots day in, day out.

"Just gotta make it three-and-a-half more years and I'm outta there."

We're on the Kennedy now and she groans loudly every time we're slowed by the (very typical) Saturday afternoon congestion. She mutters half-audibly about not making it on time to wherever it is she's headed. Then she starts telling me how she would've never taken the expressway.

"I'm a driver and I never get on the highway. I can't be having this. No."

I explain to her that in my eight years driving a taxi in Chicago, I've tried every possible route from Wicker Park to downtown and that I have no possible interest in having her in my taxi even a moment longer than is absolutely necessary.

One good thing about some people is that they don't ever catch on when they're being insulted. She just keeps talking.

A couple times before we reach Marina City, she questions what street we're on (usually moments after ordering me to take said street). After what seems like hours, we finally climb the steep ramp between her building and the Hotel Sax. The fare is $12.25. She hands me a $20 and says, "Take off $13." It's more than I expected. I wish her a good evening and she grunts something not-entirely unfriendly in response, gathers her shopping bags and climbs out. I watch her walking, shaking her head at whatever slight the world's thrown at her in the moments since leaving my taxi, then I drive down the ramp to Dearborn and away.

I wish she could've found her way home some other way.

TAKE A CHANCE

"I'm gonna take a chance," he says in lieu of a destination. When I ask where this "chance" might be, he explains: "No, now wait. I'm thinking of going to this one location and knocking on the door and if this individual isn't there, I'll need to go right back here. Otherwise, I go home to my wife. I live just up the street."

I ponder what he's saying for a moment. It's been a slow night and there hasn't been much trouble as of yet, so, what the hell. "I'll need you to pay me before you get out of the cab to knock on that door, okay?" I tell him.

He agrees and we head east on Chicago Avenue. Less than two blocks pass before I hear him feeling about on the seat and he says, "Oh no, we gotta go back. I forgot my dissertation at the bar. I'm a PhD candidate at DePaul. I'm dead without that thing!"

After retrieving a small zippered case from the bar, we're back on track, south on Western Avenue to the Eisenhower. Our destination is 49th and King Drive. He asks if he can smoke and I tell him I'd rather he didn't, explaining that it's a new cab and I'm trying to keep it that way. "What if I really have to?" he persists.

"I'll take you back and you can take another cab," I answer.

He's quiet, then wants to know, "Can I take a leak before we get on the highway?" We pull in back of a darkened Popeye's and he relieves himself. We catch the Eisenhower at Congress and go east, then switch to the Dan Ryan. He's passed out now which is just as well because I have no desire to talk about where he's going.

There's not much stirring on 47th Street at 3:30 in the morning. A gas station near Wabash seems the only thing open. We keep on to King Drive, then turn south. I tell him we're almost there in a raised voice, and he stirs awake. King Drive is a boulevard from McCormick Place all the way to 51st Street, so we swing around to the access road and stop in front of a shuttered-looking greystone. He's growing a bit agitated now. He hands me his debit card and I run it for $25. He sprints up the steps and knocks on the door. A light goes on and the door opens a crack. He comes back, and I hand him his card and receipt.

"Now I gotta go in there and I'll be out in like, five minutes," he says, digging through his pockets, coming up with two fives, and handing them over. "You're not hearing any of this are you? You're gonna take off, aren't you?" he looks panicked.

"It's now 3:55. If you're not out by 4:00, I'm gone," I say. He starts back toward the house, looking over his shoulder twice before disappearing inside. I pull into a parking spot with unobstructed views of the doorway, as well as the sidewalks in either direction. He's back within three minutes.

"Well, that was a waste. Can you take me back where we came from? Can we stop to get cigarettes on the way too?" he says, then puts on his headphones and tilts his head back. His music is audible over my stereo. It's all about niggaz and bitches and it's punctuated by multiple rounds going off. Better in his ears than through my windshield. We head north on the Ryan.

We exit at Augusta and go west to Western and pull in at the BP. Turning on the light rouses him; his eyes are now wide open as he pops out to get smokes. His place is a few blocks further west. He hands me the debit card again and I run it for $22 as he thanks me for being cool and taking care of him. He waves and gives me a thumbs-up while lighting his cigarette and crossing the street. I hope the chance he took was worth it.

 irst dates, flirtations, hookups, breakups, hostilities, and heart-breaks all happen during cab rides. Ferrying lovebirds to and from the places they make love is a particular joy of this business.

GIRL AND THE GOAT

Early in the evening two couples—two men and two women—ask to go to the restaurant The Girl and the Goat. They spend the whole ride from Ukrainian Village to the West Loop talking about sleeping habits. One of the guys tells about the heating pad they have that goes under the sheets. He says the mattress is ice-cold on winter nights despite the rest of the bedroom being balmy. One of the women goes on at length about night sweats that leave her tee shirts soaked. Her girlfriend confirms this. One of the men suggests a solution: "You should get Botox all over your body to block all your sweat glands!"

PROM

Five Hispanic girls squeeze in. Their boyfriends tell them the address of the club, waiting in the street for the next taxi to happen by. There's a lot of laughter, the kind only a group of girls on a night out can make.

One starts telling the others about her boyfriend, Aldo, being stuck talking to her father all night. "So you know how my father's kind of a racist, how he's always making those awful jokes? He kept talking about how he only goes to Hooters for the food, and Aldo had to play along, poor guy. He just kept nodding, you know? Agreeing, right?

"Then my dad starts talking about how he likes to slice Guatemalans and Aldo doesn't know what to say, but that's how my dad pronounces 'watermelons,' you know?"

The other girls are howling. One of them says, "I know exactly what you mean. *My* dad says 'marshmallow' when what he means is 'mushroom!'"

RIVER NORTH

River North is thick with nightclubs. The epicenter is the intersection of Ontario and Franklin. On a weekend night the normal four lanes leading to the highway are choked down to one due to a glut of outsized four-wheeled monstrosities waiting to be valet parked, or just idling to preen in front of one another. Every few years, clubs with names like Crescendo, Ontourage, and Tsar open, burn bright for a bit, then close. I've never had the slightest temptation to go into any of these places.

A balding and tired man named Dmitry and his two much-younger, barely-clothed female companions take my cab to Crescendo. He seems bored and they're grimly cheerful. Likely as not, the girls are on the clock. They all speak Russian, thinking they won't be overheard, but even in my mother tongue what they're talking about doesn't really register. They seem to be going through the paces of a "wild" night out, perhaps trying to live up to something they'd seen on TV.

* * * *

A couple guys get in at Dearborn and Illinois, obviously coming from Underground, up the block. They give an address in Boystown and go back to their argument.

"Why do you always act like you don't even know me when we go out?"

"What are you talking about? Give me a break, one of my celebrity crushes was there. What did you want me to do?"

They're quiet for awhile, until we exit Lake Shore at Belmont.

"I'm gonna wake up Shel."

"Why?"

"Because I met Joe Jonas tonight. Or, I... touched him."

"I wish I could still make you feel excited the way meeting him makes you excited."

At Halsted and Roscoe, one gets out and slams the door, not waiting for his boyfriend, who pays without thanking me for the ride and slams his door as well.

At 5:30 on a Sunday morning, I'm on Ontario, headed toward the Dan Ryan and home after a long night, when another taxi pulls even on my left at a red light, just past the Rock-n-Roll McDonald's. Two women are in the backseat and the one nearest asks how my night was.

"Fine," I say, "And yours?"

"Would you like to see my friend's tits?" she asks.

I don't answer one way or the other, but the friend yanks her halter-top down anyhow. I thank them as the light turns green, wondering how many times she'd done that, or something like it, in the hours before her cab ride home.

I still don't understand what's being bought and sold in these clubs—though I know a ton of money crosses the bar. There's a decadence to it all. Bored people looking for something to shake them awake, some novelty to make them feel alive. They'll be at it again next weekend and I'll be out there too, wondering why.

FLOWERS

I pick him up at a bakery in Humboldt Park late on a Sunday night. They often call for cabs and I'm bracing for the guy I've taken from there several times before, the one with the lazy eye, who goes on and on about all the bets he makes on football and always asks for my card so he can call me all the time. It's not him.

The man has a pockmarked face and a matching black shirt-and-pants outfit with elaborate curlicue embroidery running all the way past the knees. He sighs and asks to go to Pulaski and Wrightwood. I ask if he's just getting off work and he says no, but that it's been a long day.

"Get this—my ex was graduating and I went to give her flowers. It wasn't like *that*, just friends. I found out she was cheating on me with this guy called Sergio, and he was gonna be there and I was cool with that. I wanted to let her know we were cool and all."

He asks me to stop at the 7-Eleven at Milwaukee and Fullerton. He comes out with a tallboy of Bud Ice and a pack of Newports, gets back in, and continues his story.

"So I'm waiting around downstairs—it's at the Grand Ballroom at Navy Pier—and there's no one else there except for this other dude with flowers. We get to talking and he says, 'Waiting for my girl,' and I say I'm waiting for someone too. Then he says, 'Damn Victoria, she's always late,' and that freaks me out 'cuz that's my girl's name. Sure enough, same girl. He's been with her for two years; I was with her for a year-and-a-half 'til last month; she was cheating on both of us with Sergio.

"I say, 'If you don't mind my askin', do you use a condom with her?' and he says 'No,' and I say, 'Me neither, damn.' He says he knows she cheats but doesn't care; he loves her anyway. I feel bad for him because she got money off him, too. She only came to me for sex."

He's quiet for awhile and doesn't really respond when I say it's probably a smart move that he broke it off with her.

"I'm a king. I'm faithful. You cheat on me, God bless, I deserve better than that. I loved her as hard as I could. I'm just gonna go inside and finish getting drunk."

He has me pull over at a stop sign, pays the fare, and wanders to a bungalow across the street.

CHEST HAMS

She practically gets herself run over getting me to stop. Then she drags a guy away from a group talking on the sidewalk and hurries him into the cab. We're in Printer's Row and they want to go to Lakeview, so I make my way toward Lake Shore Drive.

Every time I turn she pinballs from one side of the cab to the other—hitting the door, then caroming back into her companion, then back at the door again.

"I tend to be dramatic, if you haven't noticed," she announces.

She wants to know where I'm from and when I tell her she asks if I have a good recipe for borscht. "We're both cooks," she explains.

I don't have a recipe for her.

They gossip about work for a bit. It seems he's just started there. "I have to confess something: I feel really bad about what happened last week. I was like, 'Hey, new guy, how about an over-the-jeans handjob?' Then I practically did it with you in the middle of the restaurant. So unprofessional!"

"It's alright. I was just a little taken aback," he answers.

"I'm a very forward person. In fact I have a blog where I write about my love life and all sorts of things."

"Is it popular?"

"Well, not a lot of people follow it publicly but I get *thousands* of hits a month, so I know people are reading it. One thing, fellas, when you're playing with my chest hams, realize that they're attached to the rest of my body. Some of these guys try to turn the poor things one-eighty, like a dial. My father once emailed to ask what 'cunny' meant—it's what I call my pussy—and when I explained it he was like, 'Why didn't you just say you were talking about your twat?' Me and him are two peas in a pod."

"Chest hams? I've never heard them called that," he says. I hadn't ever heard that one either.

"Like that?" she asks him—whether she means *chest hams* or something more, I couldn't say. He doesn't respond.

When we arrive at the corner she indicated, he makes a show of digging through his pockets and comes up empty. He tells her he was planning to take the CTA from work.

"Don't worry about it. Money's not a concern. I'm a trust-fund baby," she chirps while paying the fare. They get out of the cab and linger on the curb, each waiting for the other to make the next move.

LUBE

The couple stands outside Tuman's at 2:15 a.m. in the rain. They have wine bottles, several half-opened packages, and are both sipping beer from pint glasses, the dregs of which they pour out onto the sidewalk before getting into the cab.

"Where we going?" she asks him.

"My place," he answers.

"All right, but I'm gonna need lube." She says to me, "Can you take us to the Jewel-Osco at Division and Ashland, sir?"

From their unfortunately out-loud conversation, I learn that it's his 30th birthday and they're going to celebrate by having anal sex. In front of the store, she repeats to both of us that she needs to go in and get lube. "Will you wait here?" she wants to know.

"Where am I gonna go with the birthday boy sitting in here?" I answer.

She wavers her way through the sliding doors.

"Ever date somebody way younger than you?" he says."I just turned 30 today and she's... lemme see, she's 23. There's good things and bad things about that. When they get excited about something, they get REALLY excited, and you gotta kinda just go with it. Like, I don't mean to be graphic or anything, but she's in there buying K-Y because she's on the rag and she wants to let me have anal sex with her. If you've got a woman like that, it really builds you up, you know?"

I agree and let him continue.

"So, what's your plan, man? Where do you see yourself in five years?"

I tell him I don't think about the future much.

He pauses a moment, then, ignoring what I'd said, goes on. "I'm a general contractor. Pull down about 45 grand after taxes, but what I really wanna be is an architect. It's tough out there, though. Guy I work for, he'd make four mil' on his own, but with what I do for him, he makes six. But I'll tell ya, without the love of a woman, it ain't shit."

Just then, she appears, clutching a shopping bag in one hand and a gallon jug of Ocean Spray Cranberry Juice in the other. She makes it back into the cab with some effort.

"Jesus, I'm really wasted," she announces, plopping down next to him.

His place is only a few blocks away and he continues to list his ambitions—to her now—for the rest of the ride. "I know you can be an architect, baby," she coos. They take a while to get all their things together. She wants to pay with her credit card, but he slaps her hand aside and hands me some bills. "We're really awful people, aren't we?" she says. I don't know if she's talking to me or not, but I don't answer.

TRAMP STAMP

A couple flags me from the Empty Bottle. "Where do you live?" he asks her. She gives an address in Lakeview and we go north. They make small talk. Somehow the subject of tattoos comes up, and he proudly tells her that he's got four. One of which is a tramp stamp.

"What do you mean?" she asks.

"Well, you know, it's where a tramp stamp would be. It's my, like, statement of feminism, you know?" he explains.

"Huh. What is it?"

"It's kind of like a symbol, like an ankh cross. It's part of my philosophy. See, I've got a whole philosophy based on, like, this thing I wrote once. It's about providence. Where things are just gonna, like, happen to you, you know?"

It's hard to say whether she understands or not, though I know *I'm* pretty confused. We pass the Viaduct Theater and there are band vans being loaded up after a gig.

"That's what I love about it here," he says. "There's like, all these places that are holes-in the-wall where there's all this music. One day when I don't have to, like, go to work, I'll go out to see bands every night of the week. Theater, too. I love theater. I go to Steppenwolf like, all the time."

"I totally get that. I like theater too. Back in California I had a subscription to the local theater so I went a lot. It's good that way, because you already paid so you kind of have to go, right?" she answers.

As we pass Schuba's, he points at it and says, "That's where I saw Sufjan Stevens, who's like a legend in my world. After the show we were hanging out and I think he, like, hit on me. I like his music and all but not, like, *that* much, you know?"

We stop at her place, a couple blocks away from Wrigley Field. He tells her he'll take the El back home, pays for the cab, and says, "Thanks, Boss," before following her inside. I take a last look over and she looks back just then, holding my gaze for an instant as if asking for advice with her eyes, then she turns around and she's gone.

NOT UNATTRACTIVE

They cross California, then Chicago, stopping by my cab outside the Continental at about 3:00 a.m. They light cigarettes and stand there talking, and I pay them no mind, figuring they're about to go into the bar. A few minutes later, however, the fat girl leans toward my passenger-side window and asks if I'm waiting for anyone.

Her companion, a large man in an off-the-shoulder, form-fitting black dress, curly wig, and Bride-of-Frankenstein boots takes over from there.

"All right. We'll take me home first, then you. Ashland and 18th, driver."

"I don't know why I'm so out of it all of a sudden. I shouldn't be this drunk and I don't know why I'm still so upset at seeing Robert."

"You're not over him," his friend suggests.

"Maybe. But how long is this going to last? Anyways, did you see there wasn't an unattractive person in that room? Not even that person I don't like, who kept feeling me up all night.

"So out of it all of a sudden. This is why I don't smoke anymore. The last time I smoked I went blind. Literally. I had all my other senses, though, including my sixth sense. I was only able to see people by their auras. Can you imagine? And some peoples' auras smelled—well, not smelled, but they had like a strong odor or presence or something. There was one person's aura that I liked though…"

We're by his house now.

"Okay. I only have $5. I'll give you this and I'll pay for everything next time we go out."

They kiss goodnight, he leaves, and I U-turn out of the cul-de-sac and head toward the South Loop for her stop. After a few minutes' silence she asks, "How are you?"

"All right," I say. She asks a series of questions I get asked a dozen times a night: Is this the beginning or end of your shift? How long have you been doing this? When did you start today? And on and on.

It's nearing 4:00 a.m. now and I've been up since 8:30 a.m.

"Wow. The only reason I'd ever have to get up that early is if I pissed off one of my cats."

She's going to Columbia to study live sound production. She tells me she grew up on a farm in the South and misses having dogs. She wants a Newfoundland. Her place is at Roosevelt and Wabash. She gives me a $20—which just covers the fare—and hurries out, barely saying good-bye.

OGDEN AVENUE

A gaunt, middle-aged man stands outside Twisted Spoke on a quiet Thursday night, waving his arm while sucking down what's left of his cigarette. I have to swing around to pick him up. "I have cash," he says. "Can you take me to Hinsdale? Just take Ogden." The usual route would be to take the highway so I double-check and he repeats that it's what he wants. We go around the block and head west as a light snow falls.

I can see him in the rearview, holding a cell phone closer to his face, then further away, trying to focus on the tiny lit screen. "My buddies are always sending me these things about hip replacements and cemetery plots. They're in their sixties, I only just turned fifty and they make sure to let me know what's to come." He asks if he can smoke, rolls down the window and lights up.

We pass Union Park, the medical district, Douglas Park, then Lawndale, and on into Cicero. Ogden Avenue is where Route 66 used to begin and there are remnants along the sidewalks of its old life as a major national thorough fare. We pass motels, vacant buildings, and abandoned lots. The few diagonal streets like Ogden that break up Chicago's grid often take us to the past faster than the rectilinear streets that conform to the grid. The signage goes back decades in mere miles. We burrow back through the years as they lead us out of town.

"Did you miss the last train?" I ask him. It was almost midnight.

"Here's what happened," he says. "I come down here with my buddy to party with my girlfriend and her friends. Then, her ex-boyfriend shows up. They've been broken up five years, so everything's cool, but then he starts taking off his shirt and flexing his muscles and asking me what I'm gonna do about it. My girlfriend's real embarrassed and she wants me to stay, but I gotta get outta there." He looks out the window quietly for a bit, then remarks that we haven't hit a red light in miles.

"Must be a Christmas miracle!" I say.

Approaching the tollway, I spot a cop car half obscured by a thicket of trees and slow down. "Don't worry, Johnny Law ain't looking for you, he's out for the drunks swerving all over the place," he says. I explain that cops and cab drivers are hardly friends in my experience.

He's outraged at this. "That's not right! You're just trying to make a living, getting guys who drank too much, like me, home."

I don't disagree.

We pass the town sign for Western Springs, then make a left turn onto a small street. Now it's like being inside a Christmas snow globe: sprawling houses covered in snow and twinkling multicolored lights, surrounded by trees. The narrow path meanders as he directs me to make a right turn here, a left there, until I have no idea which way we're going.

We stop in a driveway with a gleaming Mercedes and Porsche parked at the end. He tips generously, then staggers toward the house.

The $60 he gives me saves what had been a washout of a night up until then. I back out, then spend some fifteen minutes circling around his fairytale subdivision. I finally find Ogden and speed back to the city.

 cab driver is often the last person late-night revelers see before going home. In the early morning hours we see people who should've quit whatever they were doing hours ago. The taxi to plight becomes a sort of beacon to guide them home.

WHISKEY

At midnight, an ill-shaven man stops me at Western and Altgeld. "I'm just going for a bottle up the street, then back to Logan, okay?" he says in a voice which betrays that this bottle isn't the first of the night. I drop him at the liquor store and wait. He comes back and announces, "These son-sabitches, charging $7 more than Costco for a bottle of whiskey, but Cost-co's shut down already, so what am I gonna do, right?" We turn off Western onto Logan Boulevard and he wants to know if I always work nights.

I tell him that I do, and he says he's surprised he's never seen me around before.

"I do what you do. I drive a cab."

"It's one of the few perks of the job: no bosses, no coworkers," I answer.

He grunts and thanks me for the ride.

HIS NIGHT TO GET TWISTED

He crosses Clark from Wrigleyville Dog, then turns around and raises one arm as far as he can without dropping all the to-go boxes. "Can you take me to Randolph and Michigan please?" He asks how my night is.

"Okay," I say.

"Well... I don't get many nights off, so this was my night to get twist-ed. And now it's late and my old lady wants me home."

I ask him what line of work he's in. He says he's in the service indus-try. A bartender.

"Where?" I ask.

"Currently I'm unemployed but I was at Michael Jordan's until a few weeks back. Great food and good drinks. No, *great* drinks, but the hours were brutal. Mondays were seventeen-hour days, Tuesdays were another ten and I didn't make any money. It'd be one thing if I was still in my 20s but I'm about to hit 40 and I can't keep putting in more than I get out of it. Know what I mean?"

"Of course I do," I tell him.

As we near the Randolph Street exit on Lake Shore he says, "Look, I'm really going to 79th and South Shore. I was going to the Metra. Wanna just take me the rest of the way?"

I say I'd be happy to, surprised that there are still trains running at this late hour. He tells me that between all the buses and trains, it can take him two-and-a-half hours to get from South Shore to Wrigleyville.

"It's absurd that we can't get around this metropolitan area any more efficiently. Know what else is crazy? I live ten minutes away from Indiana, and if I go there to fill up my car with premium, it costs me 35 to 40 bucks. I go in downtown Chicago and it'll run me 60. But you know that, of course. I go grocery shopping there and 200 dollars' worth lasts me two-three weeks; in the city it costs me 20 dollars for food as soon as I walk out the door."

"I still wouldn't want to live in Indiana," I say, and he agrees. I ask what he'd like to do if he could do anything.

"I don't know, man, I just wanna do something to help people. Nursing's about the only thing that's hiring these days, but I did that a bit in high school—volunteering in a hospital—and I couldn't deal with all the blood, piss, and vinegar.

"I saw Bill Clinton on the *Daily Show* and he was talking about how the whole system now is set up for the Republicans and Democrats to just fight and not get anything done. I don't understand it at all. Back when he was running it, it was good. Surplus, jobs, all of it. I was at the House of Blues in those days, bringing home like 800 dollars a night. I was in grade school during Reagan and Bush. I remember it was a total shit show then. It was good during Clinton. I don't know where it all went wrong. I've got no idea what happened. I'll probably end up going into nursing anyway."

I tell him he's hardly alone in wondering what comes next. It's the way it is now.

"Me and the old lady been trying to have a kid, but I'm sort of glad we haven't had luck yet. Kids are money suckers and besides why would you want to put more of them into this world now?

"The old lady's not happy though. I wanted to have a kid when I was in my 20s. My girl got pregnant and aborted it without telling me. I'd have a… let me see… a seventeen-year-old daughter now. I've used protection since then."

We're approaching the end of Lake Shore Drive, where it turns into South Shore and merges back into the neighborhood. Not many people on the streets at 2:00 a.m. on a Tuesday, save for the occasional wildly-gesticulating homeless man and an inconspicuous older lady huddled in a bus shelter.

"What I really want to do is travel. I want to go to Asia, if only for the food. I want to eat scorpion and grasshopper, shit you can't get here. You can get almost any kind of food you want in Chicago except one kind: Polynesian. When I was younger there used to be a place right on Wabash, remember it?"

I remember the sign for it: Pago Pago with the Easter Island heads, faded on the side of abuilding at Van Buren and Wabash, though something about the lettering made it look more like *Dago Dago*.

"Me and my girl went there and we ordered Doctor Zhivagos. It was great."

We get off South Shore and stop on a side street. The fare comes to $33.45 and he takes a while figuring out how to assemble his pocketful of bills into the amount he'd like to give me. Finally, he hands over three crisp twenties and asks for seven bucks back. I thank him and wish him luck getting to all the places he wants to go.

"Thanks for listening to my bullshit," he says and walks towards his house.

7-ELEVEN

At a 7-Eleven in Lincoln Park a man dressed in a winter jumpsuit with shorts over the top of itis completely entranced by the rack of energy bars. He's frozen there like a mime. His rapt gaze is about to burn holes through the tinfoil wrappers but when I pass close to him to get to the coffee machine he hurriedly moves over to the newspaper rack. He's still trying to hypnotize it as I walk back out to the cab.

LAST OF THE NIGHT

I'm second in line outside the Continental. It's 5:00 a.m. on Sunday morning; the bar lights are up all the way. The bar back can be seen through the window sweeping up. There are no patrons left inside. A little bald man in an oversize white evening coat staggers out of the cab in front of mine and toward the bar's door. He has a bottle of Corona in each fist.

Turned away from the locked door, the bald man makes his way down the sidewalk past my cab, to the one behind me. In the rearview mirror, he appears to be bargaining unsuccessfully with the driver through the passenger-side window. He gives up and lurches my way. "You take me Montrose an' Kimball?" he asks, eyes bulging out of his head. I wave him in.

Waiting to make a U-turn, the other cab pulls even with me and the driver shakes his head frantically to indicate that I'm making a mistake. But sometimes I'll take the wrong people just to see what will happen. We're a couple blocks into Humboldt Park before the man stirs to ask where we're going. "How about Montrose and Kimball?" I suggest; his eyes roll back up into his head. There's a trickling sound coming from back there. I turn to look. Thankfully, it's just one of the Coronas dribbling its contents onto the floor.

At the appointed intersection, I turn on all the interior lights and implore the man to waken. I remove the empty, tipped-over beer bottle from his lap and shake him back to consciousness. He looks around and repeats the address. Telling him that we're already there doesn't seem to impress him much. By and by, he requests to continue on to Lawrence (some four blocks north). He protests loudly as we drive north on Kimball that it's the wrong direction. I've had these arguments at the end of the night with many drunks and there's no way to ever convince them short of just arriving at the destination and paying them no mind.

At the corner of Lawrence, I pull over and stop the meter. "Here?" I ask. He looks around and points across the street. I swing the cab around to the west side of the street. He begins digging through his pockets, holding various bills and cards up to the light. He hands over the fare and two singles for a tip, yet remains seated with no apparent intention of leaving. "Time to go, pal," I suggest. He just stares through me.

I try it several other ways to no avail before he answers, "Hey, man, I no Mexican, call police if you wan'. I Colombian!"

He tells me how I'm making a mistake and need to take care of customers instead of telling them to get out. Pointing out that I was the only one outside the Continental willing to take him makes no impression. What I really want to do is punch him in the face and throw him out on the sidewalk. Instead I turn away, wait a moment, and tell him that I'm very tired and want to go home. A few minutes later he finally opens the door of his own accord and gets out.

It's nearly 5:30 a.m. and he's certainly the last of the night.

END OF AN ERA

I hear him before I see him, a chunky bald guy in thick glasses whistling for me to stop. More times than not when someone whistles I accelerate. *Want something to whistle at? Get yourself a dog.* For whatever reason I make an exception for him.

He gives a Gold Coast address and continues as if we've been talking all night.

"Yeah, so the girlfriends let the guys have a night to themselves, right? You figure: great! Let's go out and do it up, except that we go a couple feet, have ten beers and we're done. Time to go home. It's not how it used to be."

He sits there brooding about his passing youth. I'd be surprised if he's in his 30s, although he looked older from a distance. I tell him there's nothing wrong with growing up. The guys I see raging out there way past their prime are a sad sight.

"Reason we were out tonight is my buddy's moving out to the 'burbs. He's got a beautiful baby and they've gotta go raise her. It's all over. I got maybe 12 months left and that's it. I expect to be engaged or married by then. That's what I want but... it's sad, man. It's only 2:00 a.m. and I'm done."

I ask him again whether he'd rather be the older guy trying harder than everyone else at the club at 4:00 a.m.

"No, you're right. I drive a car that'd turn heads, but I don't feel any need to show it off. Especially if I'm going out drinking. To tell the truth, I'd rather just hang out with my girlfriend. Is that weird to say?"

"Not in the least," I assure him. Then he tells me about her labradoodle. He seems relieved to talk about domestic things.

I ask what time he gets up in the morning, and he says 6:00 a.m. "Is it any wonder you're done at 2:00 a.m.?" I wonder and he can't disagree.

Then he starts recounting the Good Old Days. About all-nighters and heroic amounts of beer. I'm compelled to console him even though nostalgia's never been much of a hobby for me. I tell him there's a time and a place, and that he'll always have those memories to savor his wild youth; that they're best left in the past. This pacifies him until we reach his place.

"Thanks for letting me vent, man. It's my busy time at work anyways. No time to be out 'til all hours. I'm an accountant."

The tip he leaves makes me wish *I* had someone to vent to.

LAUNDRY NIGHT

It's 11:45 p.m. on a Wednesday, and I'm waiting on a fare to come out of a house in Humboldt Park. The Gandalf says, "house in the back" after listing the address. I sit there, getting no response from the dispatcher as to when the party might grace me with her presence. In the mirror I see another cab creeping up and stopping. It's from a different cab company. This is a small side street so there's no doubt that he's here for the same people. In neighborhoods where cabs are hard to come by frustrated riders will call every company and take whoever comes first. We don't acknowledge one another, both waiting to see how this plays out.

A black kid in long shorts and a flat-billed ball cap level with his eyes walks out of the gangway and leans into the other cab's window. The cab peels out moments later and disappears down the street. The kid turns back toward the house, then hesitates and comes toward my cab.

"If you here for my ma, you gotta go around back. That's where the house is at," he says.

I tell him cabs don't usually do alleys—it's a good place to get jumped—but the kid insists that the operator told him the taxi would come around back. I take a deep breath and say "Fine." Sometimes I just can't help wanting to see how a thing will play out.

At the back gate, the kid reappears hauling two laundry bags that are almost as big as him. "Got more?" I ask, and he nods, breathing heavily before sprinting up the unlit passage in behind the house. I look around while he's gone, noting the elaborately-graffittied via-duct at the foot of the alley, scanning for breaks in back gates and walls whence unwelcome strangers might appear. Nearly ten minutes pass-before a girl in pink pajamas and a boy in a dark blue sweat suit come out, each struggling with a large trash bag full of clothes. They're a few years younger than the first kid. They run, skip, and jump back into the darkness. The trunk is now full of laundry. I start the meter and keep waiting.

Fifteen minutes crawl by and the kid reappears, this time with two grocery bags full of detergent and a styrofoam to-go platter of what smells like left over chicken. He puts it all in the back seat. I tell him that I've been waiting on his mother for nearly half an hour now, that the first ten minutes were free, but that she already owes me $8.65.

"Dang. She coming," he assures me and runs back in.

I hear screaming back and forth between several voices before a tired-looking, haphazardly-dressed woman appears with the two young-er children. They're carrying three or four more bags, which we stuff into the back seat.

"Where he at?" she demands of the little boy. "Go get him right now!" Then, "I'll tell you, this kid, goddamnit. I tell him to have all the laundry ready for when I get home from work. I get here and you shoulda seen the place. Clothes scattered all over the place. He piss me off so much. I'm sorry."

She settles into the front passenger seat while we wait for the kid to show up. When he does she lights into him. "You know I only got 20 bucks for the cab ride there and back. Who gonna pay for it, huh?"

He silently crawls into the back seat among the pile of laundry bags and we shove off. They're going to an all-night laundromat about a mile and half from the house, but the fare is already almost eighteen dollars. The kid and I unload all the bags quickly, making a small mountain by the laundromat doors. She doesn't move a muscle. When I get back behind the wheel she hands me a twenty. I give her two singles. She hesitates a moment then hands one of them back.

"That's for helping with all that," she says, finally moving to get out of the cab. "Thank you."

SO HOW ABOUT YOU?

On Lincoln Avenue, past Western, a guy smoking outside a quiet-looking bar puts up his hand for me to stop. "Got 30 dollars for you to go to Addison and Narragansett. Can you wait ten minutes?"

I nod and watch him flick his butt into the street and go back inside. I don't usually agree to flat-rate deals, but the one he offered was at least ten bucks in my favor, so what the hell? It's almost 3:00 a.m. on a Saturday. After the regular bars empty out there's usually a lull until the late-night drinkers have to go home at 5:00 a.m. And 30 bucks is 30 bucks.

Looking through the window, I see only a couple people toward the back of the tavern. Another cab pulls up behind me for a few minutes. Hacks always think that other cab drivers are onto something and linger close by to see if they can get some of it as well. He leaves after seeing there's not much of anything stirring here. My guy comes out a little later along with two other guys and a girl.

"We're gonna have three stops. First is just up the street at Western and Wilson, then you'll drop me and my girl there at Austin and Irving, then take my pal wherever he's going. Cool?"

I nod.

"Can we smoke in your cab?"

"Sure," I say. Normally it'd be no but I'm driving a replacement jalopy rather than my regular car (which is in the shop) so I don't care as much about keeping it nice.

They pile in and all seem to light up at once. He hands me a twenty and a ten and sits up front.

"So how about you?" he says.

"What about me?" I answer.

"How's your night?"

"All right. Yours?"

We're interrupted as his friend gets out at Wilson, offering to kick in a few bucks. He waves him off, saying it's taken care of. They say goodbye and he gets back to what he was about to say.

"Better. I've been laid off for almost a year but just got hired on at CTA. Union electrician, so it's a shitload of money all at once then nothin', y'know? Went to Maifest, had some beers, some shots, then this bar."

"Is this your regular spot?"

"Nah. So how's driving a cab? You know you're not something I see every day. Like a white guy driving a cab. What's up with that?"

I let it hang there unanswered. He sucks on his cigarette and stares cloudily ahead. The two in the back are having their own conversation. This cab has a partition so they're separated from us in a way I'd forgotten about. I haven't driven a cab with a partition in about a year and a half.

Near Austin on Irving, I ask for further directions. He tells me to turn left, go three stop signs, and then pull over.

"I gotta say that was the smoothest cab ride I ever had. You get these A-rabs, it's slam on the breaks, gun it, slam on the brakes, y'know?" he says when we get there. The girl in the back gets out and joins him. He hands me two sweaty singles and asks me to take his friend home.

"Keep going south. I'm near School and Natchez," the guy in the back says.

I ask him how his night had gone.

"Oh, all right. That girl in the back with me? She introduced me to some of her girlfriends, and I could tell some of 'em wanted to get with me but I held off, you know, being respectful and all. Then this guy tried to start some shit with me. What was he thinkin'? Couldn't he see me? I'm all tatted up, I'd have fuckin' destroyed him."

I look back at him for the first time. He's covered in tattoos and his reddish hair's in a close-cropped buzz cut. A little puffy, probably in his 30s. An old skinhead still seething with some youthful rage.

"One thing I know about cab drivers is they gotta be smart, remembering all those addresses, the whole grid. Every cab driver I meet is smart. So why are you doing this, driving a cab?"

"I needed a job," I answer.

"Is it something on the side? Do you do something else too?"

"Not much time for anything else with these hours."

"I gotta ask: do you hate it?"

"Sometimes I do, sometimes I don't."

"See, I'm actually an architect. I went to architecture school but I'm a manager at Jewel and I fuckin' hate it. Some days I can barely stand coming in to work."

We get to his address and I thank him as he's getting out of the cab.

"No, man, thank you! Be safe out there, okay?" He hands me a few bills, shakes my hand, and stumbles away.

egular customers never made it into the pages of *Hack*, though I certainly had my share. My thinking was that writing about them might be a breach of privacy, not to mention a strain on personal and professional relationships. It's also harder to have critical distance and see a subject clearly when there are close ties. Most of them were musicians and artists working late night bar hours. No one took better care of me than these people. They rescued me on dead nights more times than I can remember. A couple of them called several times a week for years; they started as passengers and ended as friends.

INCENTIVE FARE

From 2004 to 2008, most of my afternoons started with a trip to Back of the Yards. Named for the Union Stockyards, which famously made this city "Hog Butcher to the World" until they were shuttered in the early '70s, it's not the most posh neighborhood in Chicago. Boarded-up houses and young men hanging around corners eyeing passersby are commonplace, but as in most economically troubled parts of town there's much more that happens without garnering much notice. St. Rose's School at 49th and Hoyne brought me there.

The RTA (Regional Transit Authority), which regulates handicapped vans and other transport options for developmentally disabled teenagers and adults, contracted Chicago cab companies to handle some of the work the vans couldn't handle. It was called the Mobility Direct program. Many more people waited for rides to and from home than they could handle. Unlike regular cab rides, these were flat rates determined by the length of the trip—most were either $13 or $21. The passengers were also required to give the driver the cost of a bus or train ride in cash. At the end of the ride, the driver would key in a drop-off code into the Gandalf terminal and be paid out by his company's cashier a day later. It was steady, predictable business, worthwhile for slow weekday afternoons.

St. Rose's is one of the places in Chicago where the developmentally disabled spend their days. Some of these places are church-run, others city-run, and what goes on inside varies. I never went any further than the vestibules or waiting areas, and only heard about the activities therein from my passengers. Some described jobs assembling products, others described what basically sounded like daycare. The degree of their mental and physical disability varied greatly as well. Unlike so many of the people I drove around day in and day out, they absolutely needed these rides and that made me feel like my job was occasionally a bit more than just chauffeuring the bored or drunk about town.

A skinny black girl in her early 20s always made me put on WGCI (the local dance/R&B station) for her ride home to the West Side. I heard R. Kelly's *Trapped in the Closet* for the first time during one of these rides. I thought it was a put-on, a comedy skit, but she knew every word and sang along without any irony. This was the thing I appreciated most about her and many of the others in this program: the lack of irony in the way they took in their world.

Many passengers were barely verbal, but there was no mistaking whether they'd had a bad or good day. Sometimes it was as simple as a smile of recognition as they got into the cab, as opposed to the refusal to make eye contact. The impediments they were born with often robbed them of the ability to hide their emotions, at least in front of a stranger like me. I remember one guy complaining the whole way home about someone who was picking on him at St. Rose's. I never learned how the problem started, or even his tormentor's name, but the feeling of being wronged couldn't be clearer. After getting out of the cab he continued his argument all the way to his front door.

The prospect of going to the South and West Sides of Chicago to pick up handicapped passengers wasn't always that enticing to Checker drivers. Many of these passengers occasionally had to wait an hour or longer to be picked up. To remedy this, the company created an Incentive Fare competition. Each month the drivers who picked up the most fares that had been waiting half an hour or longer would win money. The contest applied to any kind of fare that stayed on the board awhile, but every month a large chunk came from the Mobility Direct program. Some drivers didn't want to go anywhere but downtown or the airports, others were put off by having to deal with the disabled, so the contest encouraged them to go outside their comfort zones a bit. Every month, though, the same names would appear on the winner's list posted next to the cashier's window. Checker Cab #5999 always won the top $250 prize. Three or four guys, including me, usually fought over the second place $150. Some months I'd actively try to unseat #5999 but I never came close even with a tally of up to 60 or 70 rides. His cab had tinted windows and other custom detailing. He obviously owned it and wasn't a renter like me. But I never talked to him or found out his secret to always snagging first place in our little contest. Was it altruism or just a sharpened sense of competition that drove him, or the rest of us for that matter?

Was it wrong to profit from our customers' need?

When Checker was swallowed by Yellow Cab, the Incentive Fares disappeared. The Mobility Direct program continued but seemed to be much reduced. I no longer found myself by the viaduct on Hoyne just north of St. Rose's every afternoon, waiting for 2:30 p.m., when the center would empty for the day, its occupants streaming out of the front doors to the waiting sedans, handicapped vans, and taxis.

Driving a cab felt a little less worthwhile after taking the disabled kids was no longer part of my regular routine.

NICK DIGILIO

In 2005, maybe 2006, I was searching the AM dial for something to keep me company while driving through the nighttime streets. Pausing at 720 AM, I heard an excited voice in the middle of a rant. It had a distinc-

tively Chicago cadence. I kept listening because he was debating with his listeners about what was—and was not—a zombie.

I'd never listened to WGN much. They are best known for their baseball broadcasts, and I hate the Cubs. Most of the station's other programming seemed to be geared for the geriatric set. Even though my folks would never describe themselves as liberal, I grew up with NPR in the house. The idea of listening to a commercial talk radio station had never occurred to me before, but my hours behind the wheel begged for a soundtrack, and the music stations were just unbearable. WBEZ was phasing out its great overnight music programming, replacing it with repeats from the daytime, the BBC, and other international news-related fare. Most of it bored me silly. Much of the AM dial was dominated by screaming troglodytes. Be it sports, politics, love, or gardening, there was rarely a voice that rose above the barely literate din. WGN was less offensive than most, but it put me to sleep more often than not.

But the guy debating zombies was another story. (Yes, the controversy concerned whether fast zombies were better than the classic slow ones. And, furthermore, whether the fast ones were zombies at all).

His name was Nick Digilio, and I quickly became a regular listener. His show was on Friday, Saturday, and Sunday nights—so he was there to help me ferry the drunkest fares of the week. I found out later that he'd been on WGN for some 25 years. As the progeny of Soviet intelligentsia—and an art-school graduate to boot—I disdain most pop culture by default. But hearing someone describe the latest episode of Gilmore Girls with unabashed glee and without a trace of irony makes even the biggest snob lighten up—if only for a moment. That's the joy of Nick's show.

I'd never wanted to meet any artist, musician, or other public figure particularly. Admiring what someone does, then seeking personal contact with them is quite a leap, and, often an unpleasant one. But for whatever reason, after listening to his show for a couple years, I wanted to meet Nick. I made sure to be around Tribune Tower when his show was ending. Then, I'd casually roll by and pick him up as he exited the building, as if it was just by chance. I'd seen *The King of Comedy* many times and knew from listening that Nick was a big fan of the film as well, but I wasn't trying to act like one of the obsessed fans in that film. I didn't let on that I was a fan until I drove him up to Simon's—his favorite bar—at least five or six times. I didn't want to spook him. How do you explain that you're a fan and not a stalker?

After finally introducing myself, we quickly developed a rapport. The cab rides soon became intentional rather than random. It turned out we had things to talk about. We're both baseball fanatics (even if he is a Cubs fan). But what probably bonded us most was a love of the movies. It soon became a ritual to continue the discussion of the latest films as we drove to Simon's up Lake Shore Drive in my cab. We disagree more often than not, but it's always a kick to bat around takes on the latest Coen brothers flick or debate whether Lars Von Trier is a genius or just a pompous jagoff. I remember getting a text from Nick at 4:00 a.m. once, saying that after seeing *Southland Tales* for the third time, it finally clicked for him why I loved that film so much.

In 2006, Nick invited me to be a guest on the show to talk about my writing and artwork. I'd never been on air before and had a horrible toothache (which turned out to require a root canal the next day), but Nick still made a complete novice feel at home in front of a microphone. He's gifted at providing a setting in which talk can flow. And he's the same off-mic as well—he thrives on banter. As one who's often socially ill at ease, I envy what he can do so naturally.

Nick had been involved in storefront theater for years as a founding member of the Factory Theater. He hadn't done a play for a while until *Black and Blue* in 2011. Driving him from WGN to rehearsals for weeks before the show opened revealed another side to the man. This wasn't the guy who'd go on and on about the *Jackass* films or that night's *Seinfeld* rerun. He was directing the play as well as rewriting the script and it was taking up every spare second he had. He was committed to getting it right. The piece is a comedy set in a tavern and concerns two brothers, one a Cubs fan, the other a Sox fan. It was hilarious and sincere and displayed a lot of Nick's personality. It was a true pleasure to see my friend's work on stage, to see Nick doing his thing rather than just reviewing or reacting to the work of others.

I never thought I'd know one of the voices coming from the radio. Not only do I know one now but he's even let me be part of the show.

Anybody who has been involved in Chicago's creative scene for a length of time has crossed paths with Tony Fitzpatrick. I remember his World Tattoo Gallery on South Wabash from when I was a painting student at School of the Art Institute of Chicago in the early '90s. It was a large exhibition space in an area of town that was sparsely inhabited at the time. If I'd had any concept of the art world and the way it worked, it might've behooved me to spend more time there to learn a bit about working artists and the ins and outs of conducting a career. I didn't. The concept of an artist making a living off his work seemed but a pipe dream. Instead of making a go of it, I moved back to Boston with my BFA and got behind the wheel of a cab.

Later, Tony maintained a storefront studio on Damen Avenue in Bucktown for many years. It was on one of my regular circuits around the city, so occasionally he'd flag me off the street. I knew who he was, of course, but it's never been my way to break the ice with strangers—especially well-known ones. The rides would pass in silence, but he always tipped extravagantly. Sometime in 2007, I picked him up on Damen and introduced myself as we now had a friend in common, singer Kelly Hogan. It's much easier for me to start a conversation when there's some bit of pretext for it.

Tony has never had that problem. He asked what I did and said he'd look at my website. Many people make promises in the art world, but it doesn't take most of us long to find out what those promises are worth. So when Tony called a day or two later with praise for my work—and an offer to buy a drawing—I was floored.

The piece he wanted was long gone, but he wrote out a check for $500, saying, "Will you draw me another one like it, pal?" Not long after that, he was calling for cab rides regularly.

Life around Tony was rarely dull. A parade of collectors, assistants, fans, enemies, suck-ups, and celebrities shuttled through his front door. He was always at his drawing table gluing bits of cut-up old matchbooks to make a new drawing-collage, Steve Earle blasting at deafening decibels. He thrived on all that noise, and he was always busy. There was always a new show to get ready for, a book to publish, a research trip to make. He employed a crew of young artists to help him meet the deadlines he set for himself. I'd drive many of them on errands around the city when I wasn't transporting the man himself to a dinner, an art opening, or home. Dinner with Tony was often quite an event. He had his favorite spots: Avec, Blackbird, Keefer's, then later, The Publican and Big Star. All the places he went were run by friends, and he was greeted warmly on arrival. He'd walk in and always know a half-dozen diners as well. I've never known anyone better suited to being the center of attention. As someone who has taken great pains to avoid such situations, it was quite an education.

As a rule, artists aren't the most outgoing types, and that reluctance to engage with people often prevents us from making a living by our art. So to hear Tony tell visitors why they need to buy one of his pieces was fascinating. It's one thing to be sure of what one does; it's quite another to convince others that it is so. Tony's conversations were nonstop hustles—they would continue out of the studio and into the restaurant.

There were other lessons as well, chief among them the importance of a mailing list to keep potential buyers' eyes on new work as it was completed. Tony was always talking about taking the reins of one's own career, about not letting the gatekeepers and tastemakers dictate the terms. I'd pretty much walked away from the art world, but his words were a way back in—a way to participate without feeling that I'd compromised my humanity in doing so. I've never made work for any peer's approval, and that's insured my continued employment in the service industry. But here was a person who didn't seem to suck up to people—but was still successful. There was something to be learned there.

Tony included my work in several group shows at the studio. After the openings—most of which I'd spend outside chain-smoking rather than attempting to chat up potential buyers—he'd get frustrated with me. He expected those around him to do as he did, but I was temperamentally incapable of doing so. He stopped including me after a time, and I didn't really blame him. The thing about making art is that in the end we all have to do it our own way. This goes for marketing it as well. We can't force ourselves to do what is against our nature.

After two years of seeing him most every day, Tony changed studio managers, and the new guy had a car; my services were no longer needed on a regular basis. There was still the occasional run to Portillo's for a dozen Italian beefs for the crew, but the days of daily rides were over. He also converted the studio on Damen into a gallery and started working more from home. We didn't see each other much anymore. There's a reason that I've chosen cab driving for a day job: my patience for bosses and co-workers is very thin. It's a wonder then that Tony and I got along for as long as we did. In fact, we still get along. I visited him at home a little while ago to thank him for the generous quote he provided for the back of my first book. He showed me a suite of his new etchings. We had a good talk.

It's rare that an artist is gracious and giving to other artists. Often, our world is filled with outsized egos, malicious backstabbers, and piddling beefs. Tony certainly doesn't lack for ego, but he's done me many a solid throughout our acquaintance, and I know I'm hardly alone. He is unlike anyone else I've run into in my meanderings around Chicago. The rides I gave him often passed in silence but never lacked for a sort of unspoken goodwill. Driving Tony was one of the high points of my years behind the wheel in this town.

ATO held its international meeting in Chicago a couple months before I decided to quit driving a cab in 2012. Mayor Emanuel turned the city into a militarized showplace for the visitors' benefit. That and much of what else happened after my decision did nothing but strengthen my resolve to walk away. Sometimes the universe let's you know not to let the door hit your ass on the way out.

LOCKDOWN CITY

Tuesday

I pick up a well-heeled couple from the Chicago Brauhaus in Lincoln Square. The gent has an accent I can't place, but it sounds the way rich people on TV sound. He wears a navy blue sport coat as naturally as I'd wear an old T-shirt. He's well into his 60s; his companion is a few years younger and likely not the wife but probably an assistant or attaché of some sort. They're charmed by Lincoln Square, calling it a "real" neighborhood repeatedly. They're headed to the Hyatt McCormick Place so I take Lincoln south to Irving Park and turn east toward Lake Shore Drive.

Looking out the window the man remarks that Chicago is a city that's alive. I can't disagree with him. They tell me they're here from NATO to get everything ready for the meeting at the end of the week. The woman assures me the coming inconveniences—road closures, heightened security, etc.—will be well worth it for our city in the long run. I don't say anything to that.

At the hotel I wish them well and watch as they stroll inside, looking like they own the place.

The nearly nonstop news reports about NATO remind me of the yearly Armageddon-type snowstorm predictions which hardly ever live up to the hype. Unlike the snowstorms that I always look forward to, in this case I truly hope the prognosticators are wrong. The last thing anyone needs is another '68 Democratic National Convention around here.

A businessman in the Loop asks to go to Midway Airport. His secretary advised him not to return to Chicago until next week to avoid the hassles to come. We talk about the road closures. I reassure him that, indeed, Archer Avenue will take him all the way back to the Loop in case the Stevenson is closed to accommodate the security needs of the visiting dignitaries.

At Midway, there are more immediate conflicts. The gaunt man who washes windows in the taxi staging area throws down his Windex and newspapers and stalks away from a Carriage Cab SUV a couple rows down from me. I hear his angry voice directed at a driver who's out of view. A bit later he climbs into the back seat of the Yellow next to mine. I see him telling the driver his story, his hands reinforcing his points. I can't hear a thing through the two sets of car glass but it's clear he's explaining how he's been wronged.

Thursday

I start my day at Midway. The window washer walks past my cab offering his services and I shake my head no reflexively. A moment later I call him back and tell him to go ahead, if for no other reason than to hear about yesterday. I watch him work his way methodically from the front window clockwise. When he's starting on the driver's side, I get out and ask about what happened.

"Some people, they want somethin' for nothin', know what I'm sayin'? I knew when I was doing his windows that he was gonna try to get out of payin' me. Some people are like that. I get done and he offers me a dollar. Believe that? So I throw my shit down and walk away. He's lucky I'm not waiting at his house when he gets home. Should be thanking me I'm not one of those niggers sticking a gun in his face."

Just then the Carriage SUV pulls up and its driver, a well-dressed round little man, jumps outand starts hollering in the window washer's direction. "Look at this lazy liar! He won't even do the inside! Don't give him any money!"

The washer pays him no mind. He finishes his work and asks for three bucks. I give him ten and tell him to forget about that other guy. Some people just need something to be mad about. He nods, thanks me, and walks away down the row of cabs.

At the terminal, two Northwestern University students ask to go to

O'Hare. They've missed their flight and the next one leaves from Chicago's other airport. I tell them it's a $65 fare. They act put out but after conferring for a second they get in.

I wonder whether they're getting out of town to avoid NATO but it appears that they're grappling with more important problems. One kid wears a ball cap with "drugs" printed off-center in lowercase letters on the front. He pops snack-size Kit Kats in his mouth until inadvertently smearing his pristine white V-neck T-shirt with one. "Goddamnit! This is the second one I've soiled today. This is the worst damn day of my life!"

His buddy struggles to book a flight on his smart phone, paying him little mind. "Dude, let's make a pact not to mention the missed flight this weekend, cool?"

The Kit Kat kid agrees, then digs out two battery-powered propeller yarmulkes for them to put on. Soon they're laughing, all the cares of the world forgotten. They talk about the big music festival they're going to, about what they'll wear and who they'll party with. I'm pretty sure they're going to see the Insane Clown Posse.

Before I drop them off at O'Hare, my friend Tim calls when we're two-thirds of the way to O'Hare. His band, Joan of Arc, is playing at a protest in Grant Park Friday and he asks if I can pick up some of their equipment afterwards. The Park District isn't letting them park a van anywhere near the Petrillo Bandshell. I tell him I'll do it, then hang up to pay a toll on I-294.

Friday

Tim calls to say that he won't need me, that the authorities have seen reason and are letting them load out. I'm glad for him but a bit disappointed not to be part of the action, however tangentially. A couple hours later it becomes a moot point because the city tells Tim that there will be no concert, or any other event at the band shell, that night. Everyone is confused and frustrated. A lot of people ran around, practiced, and planned for nothing.

The police presence is significant around town. Every highway ramp, as well as most downtown blocks, has cops in blue manning their positions. Off the main drags, unmarked white cargo vans full of more cops line up to prepare for the worst. The atmosphere is menacing. As afternoon turns to evening, law enforcement begins to out number civilians downtown. I only go near the Loop if taken there by a fare; better to stay in the neighborhoods and avoid the possibility of getting stuck. Everywhere else around town that I go, people get in the cab and ask apprehensively if I've been *downtown* and *how bad is it?* The populace has been properly spooked by the whole thing, that's for sure.

On my way home at 4:00 a.m., I have to bypass shut on-ramps at Roosevelt and Canalport, finally getting on the Ryan at 31st Street.

Saturday

Heading downtown around noon on a Saturday usually involves sitting in gridlock from Sox Park to the Loop on the Ryan. Not this day. With all the closed exits and dire warnings, the highway's eerily clear, almost deserted.

I have an afternoon meeting in Ravenswood and, as I wait in a coffee shop doorway, a ragtag army marches east on Montrose toward the mayor's house. A little boy asks his father what all those people are mad about and it's interesting to hear the man finesse a measured explanation, masking his irritation at having their route home blocked.

Saturday's my day to make the money that wasn't made the rest of the week. So, whatever my views on the protests might be, the object is to avoid blocked roadways today and keep the wheels turning. Staying far away from McCormick Place Convention Center and the Loop does the trick. It looks like a lot of other Chicagoans had the same idea and stayed home on this day.

Sunday

I don't intend to work much, but can't resist going down to Wrigley after the Sox sweep the Cubs in their weekend series. At Racine and Addison a man in a Cubs jersey and a woman in a Sox tee-shirt ask to go to the West Side. The woman immediately asks my baseball allegiance, letting out a wild whoop when she hears the right answer. Her husband acts outraged and threatens to jump out of the taxi. They're in good spirits and well lubricated after an afternoon in the ballpark. He shouts out the window, calling select passersby fag for wearing the wrong thing. She just laughs at him. He threatens to sic NATO on people for unspecified wrongs that they've done him. He rails against "the beaners" and insists he always sticks up for white people, that he likes them. They're Mexican and perhaps this comedy routine is for my benefit but it's hard to tell for sure.

We eventually escape the post-game traffic, and near Logan Square the woman remarks on how different it is around here than in Wrigleyville. Chicago's full of different places, that's one of the great things about it. She's had it with the city, though, and she says they're moving to the suburbs next week. I leave them to get tacos at a Mexican grocery store. She tells me for all his talk about loving everything white people do, he won't ever eat their food. After driving a couple miles away, I notice the cellphone she left on the seat and double back. They're not in the store but I remember the intersection they originally asked for and catch up to them.

"YOU THE MAN!" he screams in my face as I hand over the phone. "We were just having a big fight about her losing that thing. Thank you so much!"

Returning her phone is the high point of the week.

If the intent of the mayor was to showcase Chicago to the world while NATO was in town, I fail to see how the heavily guarded ghost town he presented could have impressed anyone.

REAR-ENDED

I leave the house at around 6:00 p.m. on the Friday evening of Memorial Day weekend. My girlfriend Shay's dog Porkchop is with me in the cab. I'm taking him to stay with friends so I can drive the busy weekend nights without having to go back home to feed and walk him while she's out of town. At 6:30, just past Hubbard's Cave downtown, the traffic in my lane stops suddenly and a second later a BMW SUV rear-ends me. The impact pushes the cab forward a few feet but not enough, thankfully, to hit the car ahead of me. Then time pretty much stops for the next few hours.

Porkchop jumps onto my lap as I slowly look back and around to see what happened. A young man—Indian or perhaps Pakistani—runs over from the BMW to check if we're all right and to apologize for what he's done. Over the two hours we spend together, he apologizes many more times. Traffic begins to flow around us again and he asks me what we should do, that he's never been in one of these before. I tell him to call the police. They ask him to pull off the highway and wait for them to file an accident report. We drift slowly toward the Augusta exit, taking care not to collide with cars trying to fly by us away from work, toward their Memorial Day weekend. I doubt very much that there'll be much to celebrate in my case.

We come to rest at the bus stop on Milwaukee, just past Augusta. I don't get out of the cab, just stay there with Porkchop on my lap, looking straight ahead, seeing the ruined weekend quite clearly. I text Nick Digilio to cancel the cab ride we'd scheduled, then call Shay's friend to see if she can come get Porkchop, since I won't be getting to her house anytime soon. The driver of the BMW keeps coming up and trying to talk to me with little success. The dog being there probably saves him from a black eye. After about fifteen minutes of sitting there, I watch him hustle a woman in a colorful dress from the back seat of the BMW into a cab. I hadn't even noticed until then that he had a passenger. He comes back to me, puts down the cell he'd been talking into, and says his insurance company needs my information. I tell him they can wait until we file the police report.

More time passes. He keeps calling the State Police and not getting anywhere. He suggests we go to the police station up Augusta and file a report but I need Shay's friend to come pick Porkchop up before I go anywhere. She shows up about half an hour later. I can hear the BMW's mashed-in bumper scraping against its front left wheel as he follows me to the police station. Upon arrival it takes a few minutes for anyone to stir enough to take notice of us. When an officer finally shuffles over, she asks where the accident occurred and immediately says it isn't their jurisdiction—interstates are for the State Police—then shuffles away without another word. The State Police had told us to go there to file a report. It's good to know our police know the law this well. All the while BMW guy is trying to make small talk. I have to tell him as we walk out of the station that we aren't gonna be friends, that I'll try to be polite, but he's ruined my whole weekend and he'd better can the chitchat. He backs off.

After calling again and determining that the State Police aren't showing up anytime soon, we exchange insurance information and go our separate ways. I think he apologizes again and I feel proud of myself for not saying what I really want to say to him. My next stop is the Yellow Cab garage on Elston. The manager takes pictures of the damage and listens to my account of the accident. Because of the holiday weekend there's nothing more to be done until Tuesday. He says to go to the company's headquarters first thing Tuesday to file the insurance claim, but for now, to go to the cashier and get a replacement cab.

I've lost about three hours of my Friday night—some of the busiest hours of the week—and between that and the prospect of driving a beater around for who-knows-how-many days while the Scion is in the shop, there's little wind left in my sails. I wander distractedly around the cab lot, trying to match up the numbers on the car keys to the sad, remaining specimens left to choose from. Crawling into a Crown Vic after being spoiled for over a year by the Scion doesn't exactly inspire greatness, but I do what I can to salvage the rest of the night and end up breaking even.

I lose several more hours when the Crown Vic overheats Sunday in the 97-degree heat. I will it back to the garage all the way from O'Hare. The cashier wants to give me a replacement for the replacement but none of the potential candidates look hardy enough to survive the afternoon so I just sit and wait for them to fix the one I rode in on.

I don't know how long it will take the shop to get to #429 because the holiday leaves them with a skeleton crew. When I stop by Tuesday to get insurance information, the shop manager tells me it might not be done until the weekend because he has to pull the whole rear-left quarter panel off. It's a twelve-hour job. I thank him and drive the replacement jalopy to the Wabash headquarters. The secretary there gives me forms to fill out and then I sit and wait. And wait. Many other drivers come and go with a variety of issues and concerns—some are addressed, others aren't—before my turn comes up. In a cubicle, just behind the secretary's desk, I'm asked to sit down and tell my story in detail. I do so while watching the man struggle to input the words into his desktop. He has to backtrack every third word to correct misspellings and punctuation. It's an excruciating, glacial process. Then, after another hour has passed, he murmurs that I'm free to go.

It's likely that the company will take $100 out of my deposit while the insurance companies work their dark arts. I'll get it back eventually but no one will compensate me for all the work-time lost. An auto accident is ten times worse if you have the misfortune of being a cab driver. It's as if now that I've decided to quit, the job is reminding me afresh of all that I won't miss.

BEST CAB RIDE EVER

A row of interchangeable bars has sprung up on Division Street just west of Damen in the last few years. With each passing month they seem to merge closer together, until their outdoor seating areas form a half-block long buffer between storefronts and roadway. On weekend nights a steady stream of drinkers flows in, out, and around these places. A line of cabs often forms here—squeezed uncomfortably into the bike lane—and passing traffic must edge into the oncoming lane to get by. Two women and a man pile into my cab and ask to go to the Green Door Tavern in River North. I pull carefully out into eastbound traffic but not carefully enough for the silver SUV which is now riding my tail.

Brights blind me and the blaring horn makes my ears ring. My response is to slow to a crawl, to really give them something to be steamed about. The honking and highbeams continue until my passengers take notice and ask what's going on. I explain that the car following us seems to have taken exception to my driving. They laugh just long enough to watch the SUV cut around us into oncoming traffic, then stop short at the stop sign at Honore. The driver's-side door swings open and small, roundish woman begins to climb out. Not waiting to find out what she might want, I steer past on the SUV's right and keep going until traffic stalls another block down. She catches up to us again. She's just about to turn this into bumper cars when I manage to get by the car in front of me and gun a right turn onto Paulina. The three in the back are getting really excited now. They think it's a game. The SUV catches us a block south. The street is wide enough for two cars and as she pulls even on the left I slam on the breaks and reverse a whole block back to Thomas. My passengers are squealing with delight as if they're at Six Flags.

Heading east we cross paths with the SUV again but after a second's hesitation she keeps going south. Perhaps her rage has finally passed. We continue toward River North.

"Dude, are you all right?" the guy asks.

"I'm fine. How are you all?" I answer.

"What was her problem? Was she drunk? I saw her passenger hop out when she stopped back there."

"I didn't see that. I hope she was drunk."

"I think I just came in my pants. That was AWESOME!"

I didn't come in my pants, in fact I don't even answer, so he talks with the girls about it instead. They all agree that it was amazing. For my part, the episode saps what little energy I have. It had been one of those days when I'd gotten little sleep but had to work anyway. I couldn't afford to give up a Saturday night. In any case I don't share their glee. I'm just relieved that no one and nothing was harmed during our little car chase.

"BEST CAB RIDE EVER!" all three repeat as they get out at the Green Door. The guy makes a show of counting out an extra five singles for my trouble. Another fare hops in before I even have a chance to process what had just happened. I drive him to the Gold Coast in silence, lingering on every passing SUV to make sure it isn't her. A couple hours later it's just another crazy cab story. Thankfully one of my last.

LAST RIDE

I used to tell people that on my last day I'd crash the cab into a wall and walk away. That didn't happen. The date—June 23rd, 2012—had been settled on a couple months back so a dramatic exit could certainly have been rehearsed and executed. But instead the day turned out to be a sort of summing-up of my nine years of cab driving in Chicago.

11:00 A.M.

I'm driving west on the Ryan and have to slow at the familiar spot near Sox Park. It'll be a slog the rest of the way to the Loop. Seeing as it's my last day I decide to be a dick and speed ahead in the right lanes—meant to exit at Chinatown—then cut back in at the last possible moment. It isn't difficult since half the drivers have their heads pointed at the cell phones in their laps in stop-and-go traffic and can't begin to react fast enough to cut me off like they should.

Since I moved to south side Beverly, time spent sitting at the curve of the expressway with the entire downtown cluster of skyscrapers in unobstructed majesty has been the highlight of my daily drive. I'll miss admiring the view, but not the snail's progress accompanied by the exhaust of a thousand semis, SUVs, and sedans. Perhaps suffering the traffic is the price for this vista.

Near the Madison exit, the clog eases but after passing Hubbard's Cave we're forced to squeeze around a white minivan that's sandwiched between a truck and a semi. Its front and rear are scrunched in in a way that might seem comical if you weren't its driver (or hadn't been rear-ended in virtually the same spot a few weeks back.) Witnessing such sights day in and day out will be something I'll have to somehow live without.

1:00 P.M.

Two couples flag me on Division near Damen and immediately dive into a discussion of how drunk they currently are and how drunk they might soon be. Seems it's one of their birthdays today.

"I really want to take a nap but I'm not going to because it's your birthday," one of the girls announces.

Then they move onto debating whether their friend who got a wedding band tattoo, then got cheated on and divorced is pathetic or endearing.

Many friends and acquaintances wish me well throughout the day. Some ask for one last ride, others buy copies of *Hack* and have them delivered by cab (the final day the offer's available). It's a little astounding that this job, along with the stories I've culled from it, has actually moved people enough to want to mark this occasion along with me. There's no way not to look back over these nine years of driving a cab in Chicago and reflect, but passing all the places I've passed so many times before makes me wonder whether they'll seem different when the meter's off for good.

8:30 P.M.

I pick up Nick Digilio at the Tribune Tower for the last time. I've driven Nick more times than anyone else over the years. He's happy to find out he's #1. Happy also not to be charged for the trip. It's the last time that the ride can be on me.

Most of the rides though are typical Saturday night rides. When deciding on a last day Saturday seemed like a no-brainer—it's the busiest night of the week, the night with the most variety of clientele, and the night that most illustrates what it is to do this work. The night to see the citizens of this city at their best and at their worst.

12:00 A.M.

It wouldn't be a proper sendoff without a puker. Mine shows up around midnight. He's pushed along with his pal into the taxi by a third man in Lincoln Park. Not trusting them to be able to steer me the right way, he sticks his cellphone through the window at me to show their destination; the screen reads Hyatt McCormick Place. He walks away from them with barely a nod of farewell.

At North and Wells, I chance to look toward my passenger-side mirror which shows my passenger leaning out of the window and vomiting a steady flow onto the pavement. The driver of the Mercedes in the next lane can't make up his mind whether to watch the puker or my reaction to him. When the light changes I pull over and let the poor guy finish. I ask him to let me know next time he feels the urge. He nods and we proceed carefully onto Lake Shore Drive and south to their hotel.

Upon arrival, the one who kept his drink down gives me $30 and an apology to cover the $17 fare and my trouble (I find another twenty dollar bill on the back-seat floor after they leave as well). I wave goodbye and drive away. Two blocks down King Drive I stop and check if they've left anything else for me. Thankfully, aside from a few streaks on the outside of the right rear door, the car looks clean.

3:30 A.M.

In advance of this day several people made offers to either document my last fare or make it memorable in one way or another. After thinking about it I decide it's best to leave the last one to chance, not to direct or control it too much. A couple local journalists do end up documenting parts of this last day but I want the very last fare to just be another fare.

Outside the Continental an Englishman comes over and asks if he can rub my beard. I decline the offer but agree to drive him to River North. When I return twenty minutes later to the same bar a guy warns me he's going all the way to Wrigleyville. I sigh and tell him to get in. If there was one neighborhood of Chicago that I could take a scalpel to and remove, it'd be Wrigleyville, but that's where he lives so that's where we go. He drifts off mid-way through the trip and upon coming to he thanks me for the lift in a way that makes clear he thinks he's in a friend's car rather than a cab. The misunderstanding is quickly cleared up and he thanks me again, this time with payment and a decent tip.

I drive around for 20 minutes or so with no luck. It's nearing 5:00 a.m. now, which is the hour I set as quitting time. I take one more pass west on Division toward Damen and a girl flags me down. I take her to Lyndale and Milwaukee. The meter reads $7.05 and I look back to see her fumbling through her wallet for her credit card.

"I'm sorry. I have a card or five dollars cash," she says.

"I'll take the five dollars."

"You sure that won't mess you up?" she asks.

"Not in the least."

She thanks me and walks away. She's my last fare. I'm now a former cab driver.

On June 23rd, 2012, I take Checker Cab #429 back to the garage. It's been my cab since March 2011. I've probably spent more time in this car than anywhere else over the last 15 months.

I hand my meter to the cashier and walk out to Shay's car, looking forward to being the passenger for a while.

I never kept a notepad or recorded any of the conversations or scenes I witnessed in all my years behind the wheel in any formal way. But, from 2009 to 2012, I used Twitter to share what was happening in the cab, as it happened. Many of these short messages led to the vignettes and longer essays that comprise *Hack*, as well as this book; some were captured fragments of speech or action that were an end in themselves. Here are a few of those:

September 1, 2010—The brakes of this Buick behind me sounds like a swarm of cicadas.

September 8, 2010—A lady working for one of the aldermen told me they oughta "stagnate" their schedule, so some could go home early. Busy at City Hall today.

September 18, 2010—At 99th & Halsted: a souped-up old Regal with oversized rims (with spinners), tinted glass, and a sticker reading, "Pray For The Unborn."

September 18, 2010—Instead of calling people douchebags, my passenger's 13-year-old daughter now refers to them as "French Showers."

September 18, 2010—What I learned from the fellas: "ATM means something else, if you think about it... Ass To Mouth!"

September 24, 2010—"I'm French and British—I'm a cocky surrenderer."

September 26, 2010—Girl#1: Can we do a keg-stand when we get there? Girl#2: Oh, totally, I'm not wearing any underwear, it's gonna be awesome!

October 3, 2010—A bit of overheard advice: 1.) Use a lot of tongue 2.) Don't use your teeth 3.) Don't forget the other side.

November 19, 2010—My passengers are debating whether "guido" is pronounced "gwee-do" or "guydo"...They're going to a bar they think is open. It isn't.

November 20, 2010—"Mercenaries have to go around converting people."

November 30, 2010—He has me stop at a burrito joint, then begs some girl on the phone to have him over to give a butt massage. "It'll be good for both of us."

December 12, 2010—My customers are arguing seriously about whether "transcendental" is a real word. Then they reminisce about their college days...

December 12, 2010—"I really appreciate you being cool about, you know, everything that's going on." Then he gives me $30 on a $6.75 fare. Thanks, alcohol!

December 19, 2010—"I read all the *Twilight* books only until they fucked. Once they fucked, I lost interest and stopped reading."

December 20, 2010—This guy's regaling his date with a story about some colleague "channeling his inner Jew," then proceeds to leave me a 5% tip.

December 23, 2010—"It's okay if you pee your pants a lot, I do it all the time when I'm drunk."

December 30, 2010—"Hey, Kat—heard you think I'm drunk all the time. Well, I'm calling to say it's not true...don't pick up, cuz then I'd call incestuously."

January 1, 2011—"This guy I'm seeing, I think he's half-retarded. But, you know, that's okay because sometimes those retarded guys are pretty smart."

January 26, 2011—Yawning, he tells me, "People used to tell me it's hard to go to sleep with money in your pocket. They lie..."

January 27, 2011—"If I was a cab driver, I'd write down every conversation," the girl says.

January 29, 2011—No matter how many times I've passed those Elvis and Marilyn cut-outs on Belmont, I slow down, thinking they might need a taxi.

February 11, 2011—I love when they ask to be taken to an intersection of two streets that run parallel. I always offer to take them. No takers yet.

February 12, 2011—If you stare for a whole minute at your house and are not convinced it's the right address, it's fair to assume that you've been overserved.

February 17, 2011—"This girl I dated, we went to Wendy's and she ordered a Jubie Cheebie and the guy knew exactly what she was talking about."

February 26, 2011—"Fifteen years ago if you went to a pro-life rally, you'd be guaranteed to get laid."

March 4, 2011—Rave Girl #1: Why doesn't Alexa ever smile with her teeth? Rave Girl #2: She thinks it makes her look fat...

March 18, 2011—A girl gets in and says, "Let me tell you where I'm goin'...I don't know the address. I've been drinking all day since two days ago."

March 19, 2011—Woman #1: My fridge? A shelf of Heineken, a shelf of Corona, two bottles of chablis, and a yogurt. Woman #2: Whoa, you're like a dude!

April 1, 2011—One black girl tells the other, "Not racist or nothin', but there was too many Africans in that club and they all smelled like shea butter."

April 1, 2011—Cub fan analysis of Opening Day: "Could've been better: more bitches usually wear tank-tops than they did today."

April 5, 2011—My passenger's clairvoyant. Here's what he knows about me: I'm a 24-y.o. Aries, UIC graduate in Business Administration, and love soccer...

April 7, 2011—Two blitzed Sox fans get in and the girl says, "Wow, what a great Opening Day. I don't remember any of the game, but it was a great day."

April 15, 2011—"My neighbors had internet before it existed."

April 16, 2011—"I was like trying to get with that one guy by the window and he was having it. Then he wasn't. Got no time for that; have it or don't!"

April 22, 2011—Cubs fans leaving the game look on the bright side: "We had an unobstructed view."

April 26, 2011—DePaul Chick: I feel like when it's a white cab driver, I tip more. Isn't that true? Me: Don't know, I've never been a black cab driver.

May 7, 2011—"I want to love people but I'm so tired."

May 19, 2011—There's a man at Western & Division loudly directing traffic, even though there's no traffic.

May 27, 2011—"I'm drunk and I'm vulnerable and I'll suck dick for coke."

June 7, 2011—"So nice to have a white driver who turns on the A/C and doesn't smell."

June 13, 2011—There are days when I wish none of my passengers spoke English. Just "Gracias" and cash works just fine.

June 17, 2011—Most nights that I go to the taxi garage to pay my lease, there are cabs idling in the lot, windows open a crack, with men asleep inside.

July 2, 2011—"I wish it would rain more so I wouldn't feel social pressure to go out and do things every time it was nice out and I could stay home..."

August 28, 2011—It's 1:30am and at Western & Grace there's a girl hula-hooping outside a tavern.

November 27, 2011—"There comes a point in the night when nothing else is gonna happen."

February 17, 2012—MALL OF AMERICA HERE WE COME, WE HAVE BIEBER FEVER, & girls' names decorate the van's windows. The driver's smoking with the windows up.

February 25, 2012—"That was fun, hanging out with people other than us."

February 25, 2012—"That chick my buddy left with? She lives west of Western. Which is pretty unusual if you're, you know, white."

February 25, 2012—My passenger spent $250 on jeans and $200 on a top at Bloomingdale's rather than going home to change.

February 28, 2012—A father to his small son, "See, this area near the lake is called the Gold Coast. 'Gold' means it's nice."

March 1, 2012—"How much is a little cocaine?"

March 3, 2012—I'm trying to explain to an inebriated passenger why we can't turn left onto the street on which we're currently driving.

March 8, 2012—The old man gets in and gives me a knowing look. "I know the way the cab industry works: the Arabs run the whole thing." Oy...

March 10, 2012—"That's the Walgreen's I used to stumble to stoned for Ben & Jerry's. That was a weird year. I didn't like what happened to myself."

March 15, 2012—So strange to drive into a dense fog on Lake Shore Drive with the setting sun still clearly visible in between the skyscrapers in the west.

March 17, 2012—As we pass the BP station at LaSalle & Clark he asks his buddy, "Hey, look! Is that an Andrew Lloyd Webber?"

March 25, 2012—Some that leave the 4am bar look like they're ice-skating on the sidewalk, others like they're snow-shoeing; few are just plain walking.

March 27, 2012—My passenger believes going to the McDonald's Drive-thru & buying his wife a Filet-o-Fish Value Meal will make up for his coming home drunk.

March 29, 2012—Always eerie to drive through the industrial park where the stockyards used to be.

April 3, 2012—What I just learned from a little girl at the Speedway: "A need is something you have to have; a want is something you...want."

April 14, 2012—GIRL#1: I'm in strip-club mode! GUY: Not going to a strip club. GIRL#2: You don't have to go to a strip club to be in strip-club mode.

April 25, 2012—My passenger's going up to Wrigleyville at midnight, hoping some girl's drunk enough by now to take him home.

April 27, 2012—"My boo isn't calling. I'm gonna drown myself in a tub-ful of Klonopins..."

May 8, 2012—A man walks into the Speedway, stops in front of the rollers, takes off his ballcap & watches the hotdogs for a few seconds then walks out.

May 16, 2012—There's a lot I'm not gonna miss about this job.

May 26, 2012—A man who appears to be admiring the Chicago River from in front of the Wrigley Building is in fact just taking a leak.

June 2, 2012—Every tourist I drive past Marina City wonders, open-mouthed, about those parked cars plunging into the Chicago River. Every single one.

I don't miss it for a minute. I have no intention or itch to go back to it. I don't miss the 14-hour shifts, the constant low-level tension, the wariness of every passing cop car, the lousy pay, and so many other problems inherent to the job.

People ask what I'll write about now, what I'll use for material, but I've never lacked for subject matter. In the cab I watched and listened to people. That's also what I did before ever getting behind the wheel and what I'll do now that I don't drive any more.

All you have to do is keep your eyes and ears open and the world will never stop telling you its stories.

ACKNOWLEDGMENTS

Unlike painting, writing a book is rarely a one-man show. This book certainly wasn't.

I'd like to thank Shay DeGrandis, Martha Bayne, and Bill Savage for reading through early, middle, and late versions of this book and never failing to make it better. They each saw much that I couldn't see in these pages. Nothing better for a writer than a set of fresh eyes, and these three have some of the freshest around.

A great thanks to Naomi Huffman, Victor Giron, Jacob Knabb, and everyone else at Curbside for taking a chance on this book when others wouldn't.

Thanks to *Chicago* magazine, *The Chicago Dispatcher*, and *The Classical* for publishing earlier versions of some of these pieces.

A great thanks to everyone who contributed to my Kickstarter campaign in 2012. You all helped give me the extra incentive to walk away from the cab industry after 12 long years.

DMITRY SAMAROV

was born in Moscow, USSR, in 1970. He immigrated to the United States with his family in 1978. He got in trouble in first grade for doodling on his Lenin Red Star pin and hasn't stopped doodling since. After a false start at Parsons School of Design in New York, he graduated with a BFA in painting and printmaking from the School of the Art Institute of Chicago in 1993. Upon graduation he promptly began driving a cab—first in Boston, then after a time, in Chicago.

CRAZY HORSE'S GIRLFRIEND
A novel by Erika T. Wurth

"Crazy Horse's Girlfriend *is gritty and tough and sad beyond measure; but it also contains startling, heartfelt moments of hope and love. In my opinion, a writer can't do much better than that.*"

—Donald Ray Pollock, author of *Knockemstiff* and *Donnybrook*

Margaritte is a sharp-tongued, drug-dealing, sixteen-year-old Native American floundering in a Colorado town crippled by poverty, unemployment, and drug abuse. She hates the burn-out, futureless kids surrounding her and dreams that she and her unreliable new boyfriend can move far beyond the bright lights of Denver that float on the horizon before the daily suffocation of teen pregnancy eats her alive.

THE OLD NEIGHBORHOOD
A novel by Bill Hillmann

"A raucous but soulful account of growing up on the mean streets of Chicago, and the choices kids are forced to make on a daily basis. This cool, incendiary rites of passage novel is the real deal."

—Irvine Welsh, author of *Trainspotting*

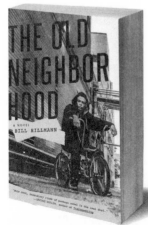

The Old Neighborhood is the story of teenager Joe Walsh, the youngest in a large, mixed-race family living in Chicago. After Joe witnesses his older brother commit a gangland murder, his friends and family drag him down into a pit of violence that reaches a bloody impasse when his elder sister begins dating a rival gang member. *The Old Neighborhood* is both a brutal tale of growing up tough in a mean city, and a beautiful harkening to the heartbreak of youth.

DOES NOT LOVE
A novel by James Tadd Adcox

"...Adcox is a writer who knows how to make the reader believe the impossible, in his capable hands, is always possible, and the ordinary, in his elegant words, is truly extraordinary."

—Roxane Gay, author of *Bad Feminist* and *An Untamed State*

Set in an archly comedic alternate reality version of Indianapolis that is completely overrun by Big Pharma, James Tadd Adcox's debut novel chronicles Robert and Viola's attempts to overcome loss through the miracles of modern pharmaceuticals. Viola falls out of love following her body's third "spontaneous abortion," while her husband Robert becomes enmeshed in an elaborate conspiracy designed to look like a drug study.

LET GO AND GO ON AND ON
A novel by Tim Kinsella

"I give Kinsella a five thousand star review for launching me deep into an alternate universe somewhere between fiction of the most intimate and biography of the most compelling. It's like...a pitch-perfect fine flowing bellow, the sound of celestial molasses." **—Devendra Banhart**

Let Go and Go On and On is the story of obscure actress Laurie Bird. Told in a second-person narrative, blurring what little is known of her actual biography with her roles as a drifter in *Two Lane Blacktop*, a champion's wife in *Cockfighter*, and an aging rock star's Hollywood girlfriend in *Annie Hall*, the story unravels in Bird's suicide at the age of 26. *Let Go and Go On and On* explores our endless fascination with the Hollywood machine and the weirdness that is celebrity culture.